REFERENCE - - NOT TO BE
TAKEN FROM THIS ROOM

Lets go see...
_____ by

"*BICYCLE*..."

Dr. Henry C. Molinoff

LONGWOOD PUBLIC LIBRARY

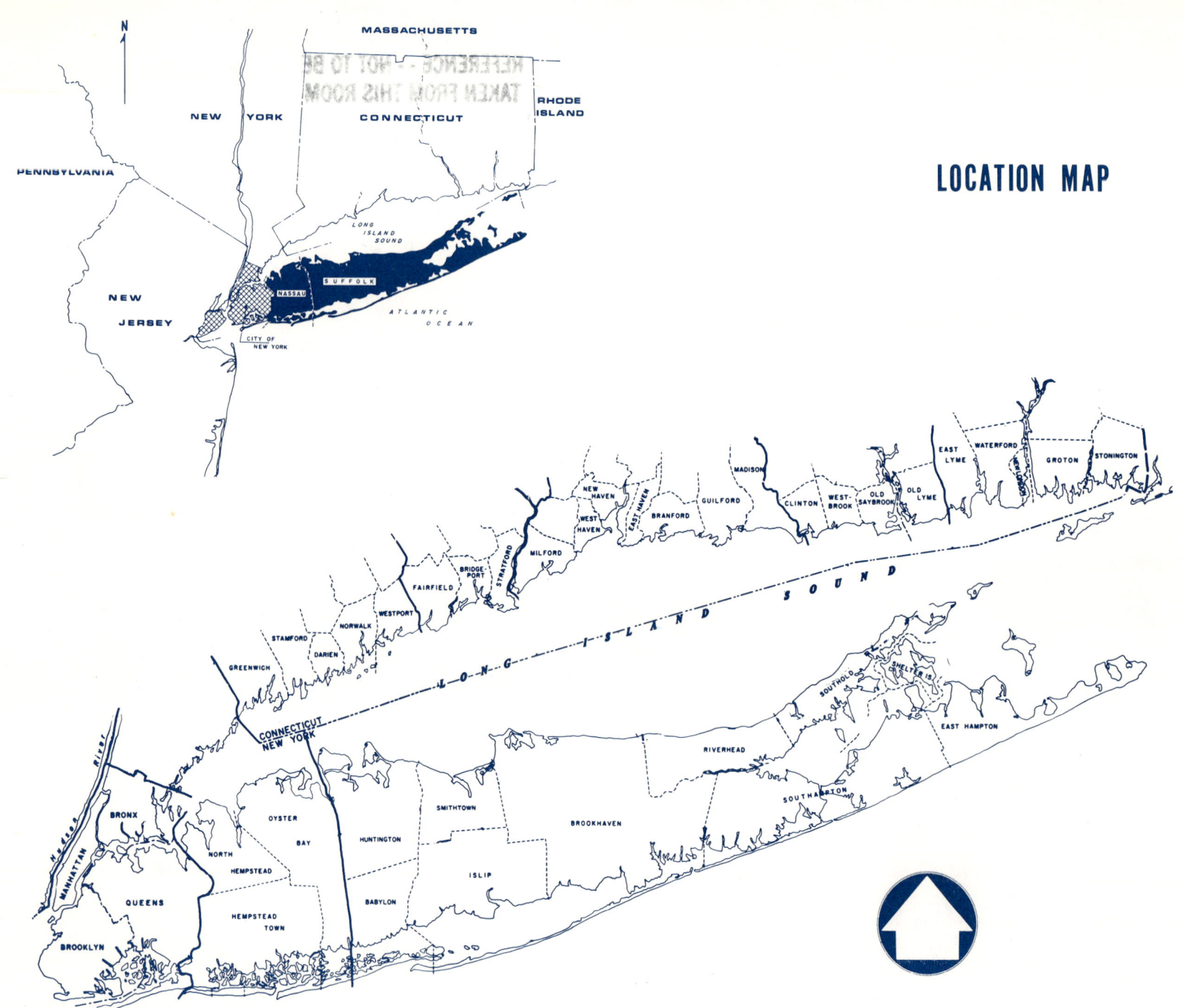

LOCATION MAP

COUNTY EXECUTIVE'S MESSAGE

For several years the Suffolk County Planning Department has promoted the establishment of bicycle trails as a desirable activity. This document, written by a distinguished Suffolk County citizen, Dr. Henry Molinoff, and donated by him as a public service to the people of Suffolk County, is exciting proof of the benefits and pleasures that every citizen can enjoy.

It is particularly fitting this year as Suffolk County prepares to celebrate its 300th anniversary that we make this book available to the citizens of the County. I hope it will serve as a challenge and a guide for citizens and visitors alike to discover the priceless natural and cultural heritage that is Long Island. We have included in this book similar opportunities to the west, which only serve to prove that this is indeed a splendid isle.

March 1983

Peter F. Cohalan
Suffolk County Executive

PREFACE

In the summer of 1980 my father, then 72 years of age, and my son, then 11 years of age, set out to bicycle from Denver, Colorado to Ogallah, Nebraska, a distance of 225 miles. My father was already an accomplished bicyclist, averaging in the range of 100-200 miles per week. Jeffrey, on the other hand, had never ridden more than five or six miles at a time. When they set out, I was prepared to pick up at least Jeffrey within 50 miles of home. Instead, they did beautifully, averaging around 35 miles per day. Of course they did not exactly "rough it." They stayed in hotels along the way, had steak dinners most nights, and at least one of them preceded dinner with a martini. Some two to three days out, Jeffrey remarked, "What a wonderful experience. We are biking 250 miles together when most people your age are already dead!" My own impression is that Ponce de Leon's stationary fountain of youth does not compare with the two wheels and a set of pedals that have transported my father. Although his birth certificate indicates that he is 74 years of age, he looks and acts as if he is somewhat under 60. Even more impressive is the fact that he appears to be getting younger rather than older.

Some ten or more years ago, my father began to suffer from episodes of acute atrial fibrillation. The condition was treated with various drugs, which to a greater or lesser extent decreased the frequency of the attack. He was never happy with the side effects of these agents, and being a somewhat independent spirit, he has manipulated his own dosage so that now he is on what is probably a homeopathic dose. Nonetheless, he decided about ten years ago that he needed a regular exercise program since the attacks of atrial fibrillation, though not life threatening, gave him the unpleasant feeling of his own mortality. The word "Moderation" has never been applied to anything that my father has undertaken. That may be a major reason that he has been so successful both professionally as a dentist and recreationally as a hobbyist. Over the years, his hobbies have included growing rhododendrons, azaleas, roses and orchids, sailing his 36-foot boat up and down the East Coast, and most recently, bicycling. When his boating and bicycling hobbies overlapped, he would bicycle in various ports of call. I believe that he sold the boat ultimately because the sea air made it impossible to keep a good bicycle rust-free.

I have already mentioned some of the major advantages that my father has gained from bicycling. Obviously, he feels well and looks about fifteen years younger than his stated age. Bicycling is also a source of continued enjoyment and pleasure to him. His usual plan is to put the bicycle on the back of his car and drive to some area on Long Island. Then he will park the car and take out the bicycle for several hours of exploring. In the course of these expeditions, he has learned literally hundreds of routes through and around Long Island. His favorites provide the subject of this book. Having a wide range of interests, his trips frequently have a destination that can be a restaurant, a park, a sculpture, a garden, or a view. His appreciation of a good view has occasionally gotten me into trouble, since my own particular addiction is running. We have taken several bike-running trips together, though these are usually a bit too short and a bit too slow for my father's taste. In any case, my father will frequently suggest a short detour for a special view or a piece of apple pie. He usually forgets to mention that the detour may be up the side of a small hill or to realize that although the apple pie adds only insignificantly to the weight that a bike rider has to carry, it has a rather unpleasant effect bouncing up and down in the stomach of a runner.

This volume identifies and describes some of my father's favorite routes on Long Island and also into and around New York City. In addition to the routes described here, he has already covered a good part of the distance between New York and Florida, pedaled from San Francisco to Los Angeles, and to California from somewhere in Arizona. It is unlikely that dad will be satisfied with volume two on how to get from New York to Florida or volume three from Seattle to Baja, California. In fact, if Volume Two covers simply a transcontinental bike trip, I will be pleased. My concern, though, comes from a clipping that I saw on his desk describing the route of the Orient Express.

Perry B. Molinoff, MD
Chairman, Department of Parmacology
University of Pennsylvania Medical School

CONTENTS

	Page
Southold – Shelter Island – Greenport	1
Southampton to Sag Harbor	7
Smithtown to Stony Brook and Setauket	15
Smithtown Vicinity	25
Northport – Asharoken Beach – Eaton's Neck	33
Caumsett State Park	41
Huntington – Historic Sites and Pre-Revolutionary Houses	47
Cold Spring Harbor – Sagamore Hill to Oyster Bay	57
Oyster Bay, Oak Neck, Bayville, Mill Neck, Lattingtown	63
Bethpage State Park to Jones Beach State Park	69
Brooklyn Bridge Area and Manhattan Financial District	75
Roosevelt Island to Manhattan to Williamsburgh, Brooklyn	85

because the sea air made it impossible to keep a good bicycle rust-free.

I have already mentioned some of the major advantages that my father has gained from bicycling. Obviously, he feels well and looks about fifteen years younger than his stated age. Bicycling is also a source of continued enjoyment and pleasure to him. His usual plan is to put the bicycle on the back of his car and drive to some area on Long Island. Then he will park the car and take out the bicycle for several hours of exploring. In the course of these expeditions, he has learned literally hundreds of routes through and around Long Island. His favorites provide the subject of this book. Having a wide range of interests, his trips frequently have a destination that can be a restaurant, a park, a sculpture, a garden, or a view. His appreciation of a good view has occasionally gotten me into trouble, since my own particular addiction is running. We have taken several bike-running trips together, though these are usually a bit too short and a bit too slow for my father's taste. In any case, my father will frequently suggest a short detour for a special view or a piece of apple pie. He usually forgets to mention that the detour may be up the side of a small hill or to realize that although the apple pie adds only insignificantly to the weight that a bike rider has to carry, it has a rather unpleasant effect bouncing up and down in the stomach of a runner.

This volume identifies and describes some of my father's favorite routes on Long Island and also into and around New York City. In addition to the routes described here, he has already covered a good part of the distance between New York and Florida, pedaled from San Francisco to Los Angeles, and to California from somewhere in Arizona. It is unlikely that dad will be satisfied with volume two on how to get from New York to Florida or volume three from Seattle to Baja, California. In fact, if Volume Two covers simply a transcontinental bike trip, I will be pleased. My concern, though, comes from a clipping that I saw on his desk describing the route of the Orient Express.

Perry B. Molinoff, MD
Chairman, Department of Parmacology
University of Pennsylvania Medical School

CONTENTS

	Page
Southold - Shelter Island - Greenport	1
Southampton to Sag Harbor	7
Smithtown to Stony Brook and Setauket	15
Smithtown Vicinity	25
Northport - Asharoken Beach - Eaton's Neck	33
Caumsett State Park	41
Huntington - Historic Sites and Pre-Revolutionary Houses	47
Cold Spring Harbor - Sagamore Hill to Oyster Bay	57
Oyster Bay, Oak Neck, Bayville, Mill Neck, Lattingtown	63
Bethpage State Park to Jones Beach State Park	69
Brooklyn Bridge Area and Manhattan Financial District	75
Roosevelt Island to Manhattan to Williamsburgh, Brooklyn	85

INTRODUCTION

Seven years ago, after my first heart episode, my Cardiologist said, "You must have regular exercise - running, jogging or bicycle riding." I chose the last and went from his office to the bicycle shop. Therapy has become a joyful obsession. My bike tours would not suit the exuberantly enthusiastic exerciser bent upon sweating and working up his pulse rate to 120 or higher. Some sweat elevation of the pulses is the natural result of a fast pace or of hilly terrain covered.

My story is for the large and growing number who find in the bicycle the modern version of the magic carpet, an effortless and efficient means of locomotion. It gives the rider unimagined scope and facility and enables him to enjoy the country, the mountains, the seashore and the city. No other means of travel can equal it. I have ridden my bike in places as diverse as the hills of Wyoming, the Colorado and Alaskan Mountains, and the narrow causeways of the Florida Keys. I have ridden the busy streets of our cities - mainly, the City of New York. And, of course, I have spent many, many hours on the roads and paths of Long Island. I find screeching traffic and country quiet equally fascinating. In the summer I usually stop at a beach at some point in the journey; the cyclist goes where automobiles cannot follow, and covers distances pedestrians cannot match. The primary goal in the planning of each trip is to cover an area of interest and to enjoy both getting there and being there.

The times required for the tours I have outlined range from a few hours, for the short ones, to a full day depending upon the area. At the beginning of each trip described, you will find the approximate distance covered. You will lose much if you fail to stay and look about you. Develop the "Let's go see" attitude. If something piques your fancy, go see, stay and examine. Sit on your bike and look until you are ready to move on.

During the early days of my bike riding, the destination and purpose for a trip was a casual decision. A trip I made often was to Port Jefferson, 12 miles from home, for a cup of coffee in the winter or for a beer on a bench overlooking the harbor in the summer. When I bought the bicycle carrier for the car, this trip gave way to longer more interesting excursions. New horizons opened and the bicycle riding changed from a doctor's prescription to an exhilarating and enjoyable daily routine. Only very, very bad weather keeps me grounded.

In the bike tours described here, both the ride and the destination are important and the trips have varying distances between points of interest. Directions call for some travel on main highways, when it cannot be avoided, but I prefer to utilize secondary roads whenever possible since they are safer and more picturesque.

Transport your bicycle by automobile to the parking area I have designated for each trip. Explicit directions head each chapter. Suitable bike racks are available everywhere. They can be permanently installed or fastened onto your car as the need arises. Be sure that the bike is well above the pavement or you will lose a wheel when you hit a pot hole or when you back up.

Trips to Manhattan should be made during business hours on weekdays, for then the city is alive with sidewalk vendors and stores displaying their wares on the public walkways. You can see hustling loners, couples sharing smiles as they go about their own leisurely business - and all the gradations in between. The din of traffic, the whistle of the cops, and the impatient blaring of horns in halted traffic makes for an excitement that the city does not have on holidays or weekends. Only the skeleton of the city can be seen then. That skeleton is beautiful however. The stately skyscrapers, the fountains, the plazas, the beautiful old buildings and churches should be circled and enjoyed leisurely.

Traffic on weekdays is a challenge. It can be coped with despite the pot holes, Con Edison's work crews, and double and triple parkers. Obey the traffic laws - I stress this - for nothing is more important from the standpoint of safety. But do not do it slavishly. If traffic is stopped for a red light and there is no cross traffic, opt for the right of a pedestrian and go on - but look before you go. Traffic is not a serious problem if proper precautions are taken.

Remember that the equivalent to a little dent in the car fender is, for the cyclist, a broken arm or leg, or worse. Do not weave in and out of traffic; I see it done by brave, bold cyclists all the time. I can quote one Air Corps Instructor who said, "There are old pilots and bold pilots, but there are no old, bold pilots."

The major chance for injury in bike riding is in changing lanes. The city pot holes and double parkers make some weaving in and out normal and expected. There lies the potential for accidents. No one has yet devised a good, permanently-installed and adjusted rear view mirror for a bike. Until one is put on the market, we will do well to dismount in busy high-speed traffic before crossing the street.

I find riding the left side on one way streets safest, since you are on the driver's side and are more easily visible. But, beware of riding the left lane on high speed traffic avenues such as Park Avenue in New York City. On these roads, get to the far right and stay there even if it means stopping at bus pick up stations from time to time. If you find yourself on a street with dense traffic, diesel and gas fumes choking, and noise at a deafening level, do not stay there - get onto a parallel street which will be more pleasant.

Use the sidewalks with care and circumspection and do not hesitate to walk your bike if the need arises. You will often - very often - make better time than the autos. On East 67th Street, between First and Second Avenues, for example, I had to ride the sidewalk for a short distance. I was riding very, very slowly; my brakes squeaked and frightened a little old lady. She came after me with her walking stick, but fortunately she missed. Such minor risks are part of the game.

Weather forecasting, though not an exact science, is fairly accurate and I make it a rule to tune in on a local weather station before starting a long trip but you will get caught in rain or snow from time to time. I carry lightweight rain gear on my baggage rack at all times. Remember that your brakes lose up to 75% of their braking power when they are wet, so keep your speed down at these times. Bicycle theft is also a major problem. It embarrasses me to say that I have had three bikes stolen. With each theft I increased the scope of my protective device and hope this last one - a pick-proof, cut-proof, saw-proof contraption, will make the third theft the last one.

On air trips to other parts of the country, you can ship the bike ($14.00 each way). It is necessary to disassemble it by removing the front wheel, the pedals, the seat and the handle bars. You can take the bike apart and reassemble it in about 15 minutes. Tie all the parts to the frame with plastic ties that can be bought at any electrical supply store. They are strong, easily applied and can be cut with ordinary pliers. You can get a carton at the airport - call them in advance - or you may prefer to get two cartons at the bicycle shop. Put the tied-together bike into one carton, and slide the second one over it as a cover, put a rope around the middle, and off you go.

I hope you will find the trips described here pleasant and exciting and that you will enjoy repeating them, with variations, again and again. Happy biking.

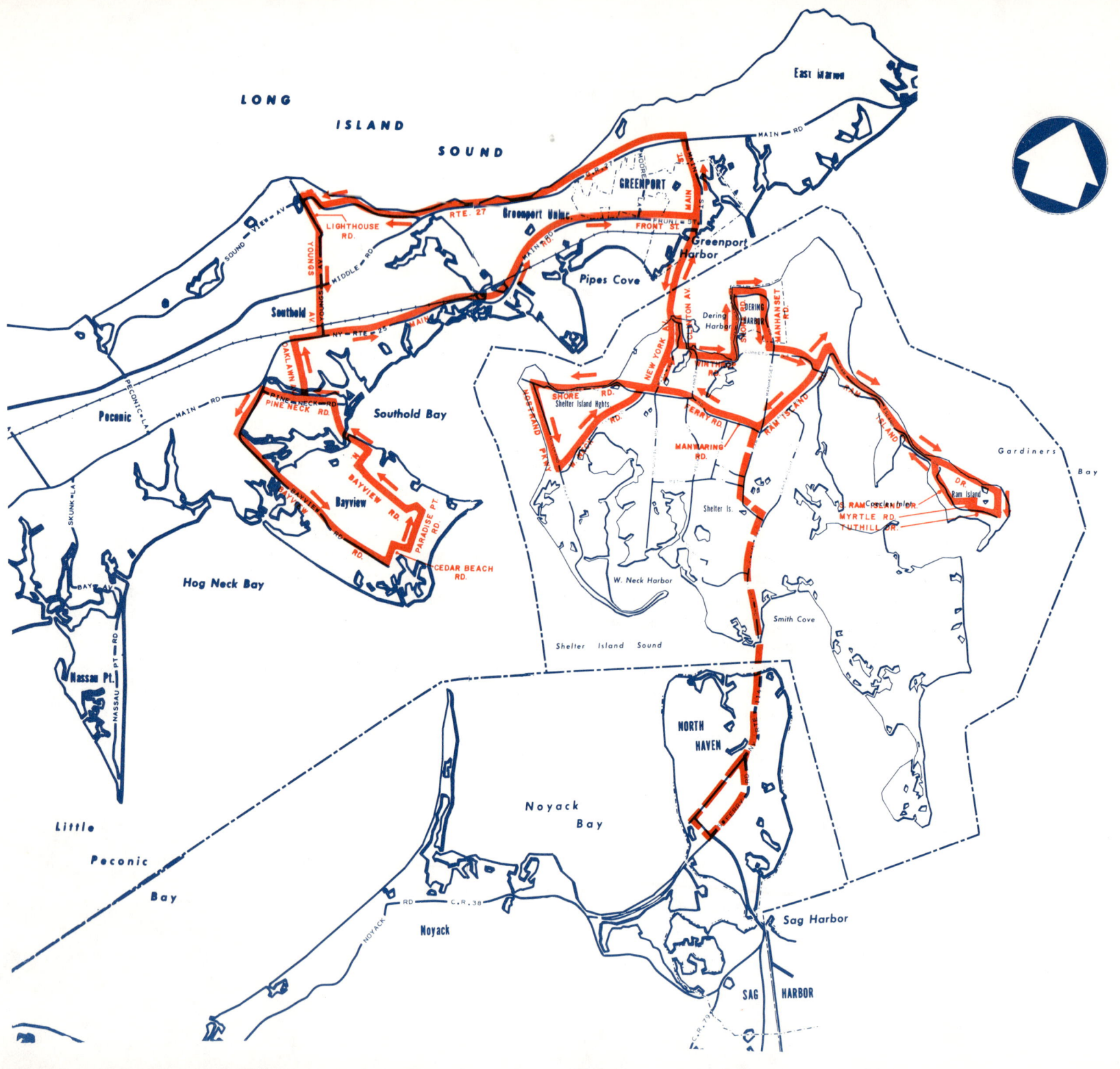

SOUTHOLD - SHELTER ISLAND - GREENPORT

Directions

Long Island Expressway to Exit 73. Go east on County Route 58 (Old Country Road) for about two and one-half miles to Northville Turnpike. Left here for two miles to Sound Avenue. Right on Sound Avenue to its merging into Main Road (N.Y. Route 25) at Mattituck. (Seven miles). Continue east for six miles on Main Road to Southold.

Southold was settled in 1640 by thirteen men, Puritans, from New Haven Connecticut who sailed across the Long Island Sound passing between Orient Point and Plum Island. Their journey took them between the North Fork and Shelter Island into the calm cove of Town Creek, an arm of Southold Bay. These Puritans and the settlers who followed them set up a town government and established church membership as a necessary requirement for the privileges of Freemen, and only they were allowed to vote.

Park your car in the vicinity of Pine Neck Road near Oaklawn or some other shady out of the way spot that you may choose near there. In my years of roaming with car and bike I have never had the car disturbed when it was locked and left for the day under a tree in a quiet residential area.

Take a bike tour of the Southold area by going east on Bayview Road to Cedar Beach. You will pass a fine old hotel, General Wayne Inn, on the way. By continung along Paradise Point Road to North Road you will complete the circle of Great Hog Neck and end the ride close to Pine Neck Road where your car was parked. Go north on Oaklawn to Main Road--the shopping area of Southold--and turn right on Main to Youngs Avenue, the third street on the right, and you will get to Town Creek. This is where those original thirteen settlers landed. Southold hamlet served as a base camp for the colonization of the North Fork. Three of the adjacent islands, Fisher Island, Plum Island and Gull Island, are part of Southold Township.

You may decide to drive the five miles to Greenport but you can bike there easily by continuing east on Main Road to Front Street, Greenport. The shoulder is reasonably smooth and can be used most of the way. There are a few occasions when pot holes make it necessary to get on the highway, and at these times do not neglect hand signals. The road skirts Southold Bay where

SOUTHOLD
*Cedar Beach County Park
(looking west)*

SOUTHOLD

*North Side of Main St.
(looking west)*

*Town Creek
(south end of Youngs Ave.)*

you will see two barges converted to restaurants specializing in seafood. The five mile ride to Front Street is intriguing and the few side roads on the south leading to the water invite exploration.

The ferry to Shelter Island can be boarded near the eastern end of Front Street, Greenport; ferry signs make it easy to find. Boats leave every fifteen minutes for the ten minute run. Fare is $1.00 for bike and rider.

The ferry docks are at Shelter Island Heights. Follow Clinton Avenue to Winthrop Road and its extension Shore Road to get to the older residential area of Dering Harbor with its marina, fishing fleet and gingerbreaded Victorian homes. These old houses line Shore Road and its extension Sylvester Road, where the Sylvester Manor House, built in 1732 still stands. It was the home of the descendant of the first settlers of Shelter Island, Nathaniel Sylvester and his wife Constance who arrived in 1652. It is and always has been a private home; unfortunately it is set far back from the road and it is unwise and unlawful to trespass to see it. They were followed soon by other Quakers who found refuge there from persecution by the Puritans.

SHELTER ISLAND
Carpentor Gothic House
(just off Rt. 114)

SHELTER ISLAND
Onboard Shelter Island Ferry
(coming into Shelter Island)

Shelter Island is one of the most beautiful areas of Long Island. The little developed countryside of gentle rolling hills of woodland and pasture with occasional views of the sea startle and please the eyes as one bikes along the never crowded two lane highways.

On completion of a tour of Dering Harbor, go south on Manhasett Road to Cobbets Lane. Turn left on Cobbets Lane to Ram Island Road. Turn left again for a very short distance and the road will make a sharp turn to the right and become Ram Island Drive. It is a two mile stretch of road with Gardiner's Bay on the left (east) and Coecles Harbor on the right with clear washed sand on both sides. Continue riding to the end of Ram Island Drive to Ram Island and take time

SHELTER ISLAND
Union Chapel - Oldest Public Edifice 1875

if you can to bike south a short distance to Shanty Bay by going right on Oak or Myrtle Street. Across the bay and closed to the public is the Mashomack Forest, 2,200 acres, owned by the Nature Conservancy to be never developed.

In the days before the massive use of DDT, many telephone poles had large circular nests of interwoven branches on their tops. These were the nests of fishhawks. The DDT in the water contaminated the fish. When the fishhawks ate them, their eggs became so thinshelled they cracked from the weight of the parent bird. Thus the birds were threatened with extinction. However, with the banning of DDT, the fishhawk is coming back. You can see occasional nests along the coast road.

Return to the main part of the island, then turn left onto Ram Island Road to Manwaring Road. At this point you can continue south on Ram Island Road to where it changes its name to Ferry Road and bike south on Ferry Road (Route 114) about four miles for a ferry ride across Shelter Island Sound to North Haven and a two mile ride on Route 114 to Sag Harbor. If you decide to limit the trip to Shelter Island, you can turn right on Manwaring to where it runs into Ferry Road, then west to West Neck Road and on to Shore Road to Rocky Point. A left turn on Nostrand Parkway will take you through West Neck. A motel and beaches can be found on Shore Road but stickers on cars are needed for entrance to the beach. What is necessary for bikes my informant did not mention.

SHELTER ISLAND
Shanty Bay
(looking across bay towards Mashomack Forest)

4

You can return to the ferry slip by going north on West Neck Road to its end. Make a sharp right, then a sharp left for a very short distance and a quick sharp left onto New York Avenue. This will lead you to Grand Avenue through Shelter Island Heights and so to the Greenport Ferry.

After leaving the ferry at Greenport take the time, if you can, to ride right on Front Street and left on Main Street to see the commercial area of Greenport and walk your bike through the dock and marina areas of the town. There are many charter boats for fishing and you can visit a marina and Yacht Clubs. The channel has a minimum depth of 35 feet making Greenport Harbor

GREENPORT
South end of Dock and Main St.
(looking northeast)

GREENPORT
Front St. (Rt. 25)
(looking northeast)

available for large ships and its sheltered waters are safe for smaller ones. The main industry of the village, centered around Stirling Basin, at the foot of Main Street is boating, either for pleasure or business. It is from here that Peconic Bay scallops are sent to all parts of the country.

You may return to your car parked at Southold by the same route used to get to Greenport, Main Road to Oaklawn Avenue, Southold, or if you'd rather, you may go north on Main Street, turn left on Route 27 and go west onto its extension, Shore View Avenue, to Lighthouse Road. Go left here until it ends at North Road. Turn right for a short distance, then left on Youngs Road to Main Road and thence right on Oaklawn to your parked car.

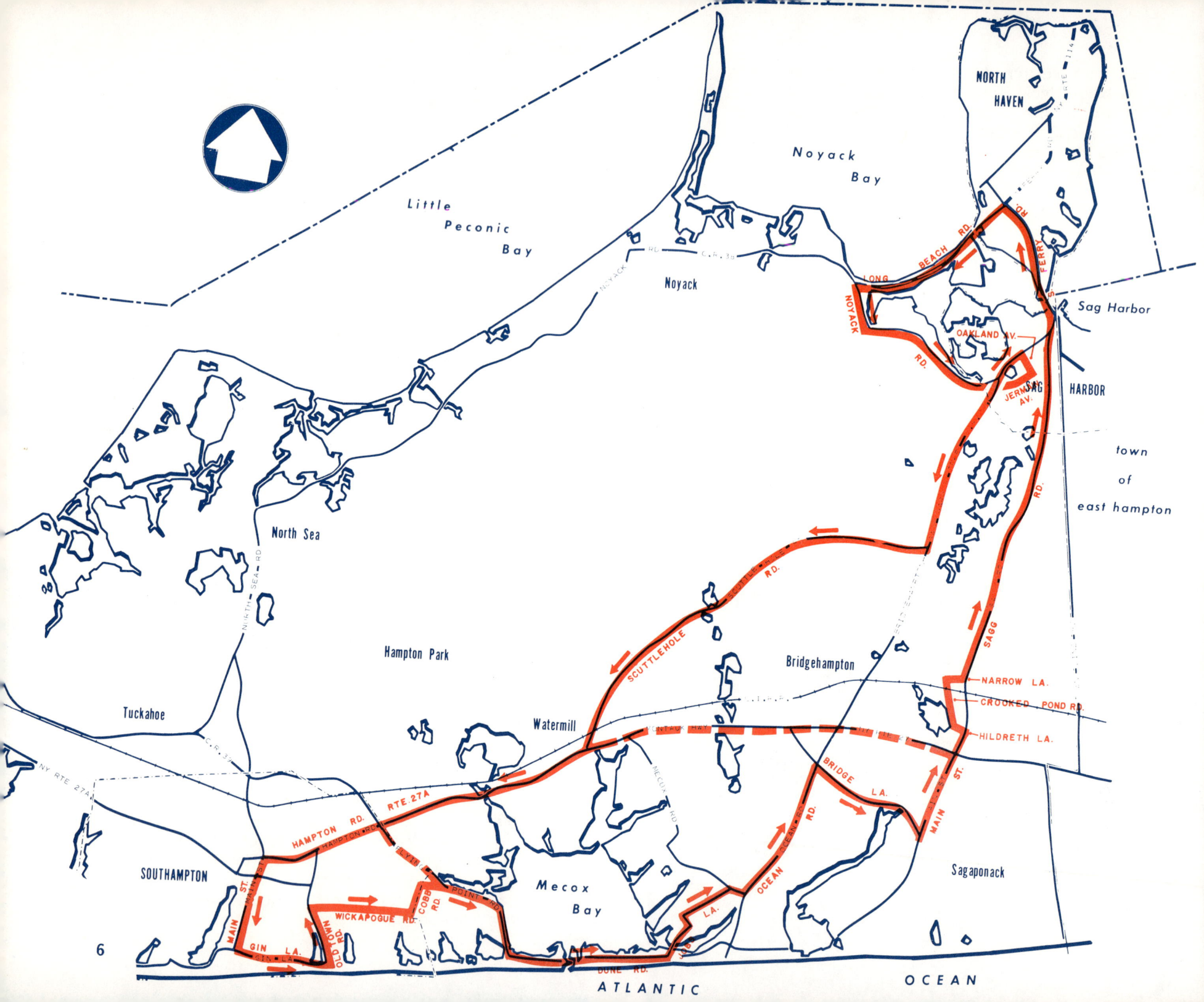

SOUTHAMPTON TO SAG HARBOR

Southampton, the queen village of Long Island, was named for the Earl of Southampton who took a leading role in the colonization of America. The first colonists were a group of eight men from Lynn Massachusetts who purchased from James Farratt, Lord Sterling's agent, the right to buy eight square miles of land from the Indians anywhere on Long Island paying four bushels of Indian corn for that right. They landed at Cow Harbor, now Huntington, but were arrested and ordered to leave by the Governor of New Amsterdam. On being released later in the summer, they sailed east and landed at Conscience Point-at North Sea. These were the men who settled Southampton at Canoe Place. They gave the Shinnecock Indians 16 coats and 60 bushels of corn to be delivered in September of 1641.

Directions

Exit number Nine, Sunrise Highway (N.Y. Route 27). Take North Sea Road to Southampton. Park your car at the municipal parking lot about 100 feet beyond Nugent Street (butts into Main Street on the left).

Distance

Approximately 40 miles.

SOUTHAMPTON
Memorial Plaque - Conscience Point

After parking your car proceed South on Main Street by bike. You will pass many distinguished stores and shops. Go to the end of Main Street and continue down the street lined with beautiful, well maintained old houses set far back from the road. Hedges, tall, old and stately give privacy and winding driveways add a charm that is reminiscent of the ante-bellum South. These old houses are interspersed with new and modern houses also set well back from the street. It is necessary to stop riding and pause at driveway entrances to get a good view of the landscape and houses behind the hedges. Turn left onto Gin Road--a continuation of Dune Road to its end at Wickapogue Rd. Turn north here onto old Town Road to Wickapogue Road to where it intersects Flying Point Road which takes you back to the ocean front.

SOUTHAMPTON
Southampton Village
(looking northeast up Main St.
from roof of Tower Gallery)

SOUTHAMPTON
Southampton Village
(looking southwest down Main St.)

You will bike past some of the most productive potato fields on Long Island. This potato crop became, in twentieth century, a major source of the Long Island income valued at many millions of dollars. It had its origin in the surface cultivation by the Indians of the "white root nut". Hybridization and selective cultivation over the centuries changed these "white root nuts" to the present potatoes grown and consumed so widely.

Continue on Flying Point Road to its end at Mecox Bay. You will pass sand dunes and hear the sound of the ocean crashing on the right and on the left you will see placid Mecox Bay, which is not a bay at all but a pond that owes its origin as does all of Long Island, to glacial activity.

When the glacier rolled down from the north it brought icebergs of varying sizes along with sand, gravel, rocks and soil. When the glacier melted, it deposited all its solid material and formed Long Island. Where icebergs lay in the glacier there was no solid material and a depression or vacancy resulted. The depression serves as a reservoir to catch the rainfall and drain the surrounding area. Mecox Bay owes its origin to this glacial action. It is called a kettle pond. This bay must be opened at its southern end periodically to drain some of its water into the ocean. When I was there a drag line dredge was busy excavating the sand to lower the height of the water and prevent flooding of the adjacent farm land and homes. (Lake Ronkonkoma is the largest of the kettle ponds on Long Island.)

At this point you can elect to go back on Flying Point Road to Cobb Road and left on Montauk Highway to return to Southampton or you can go right (east) on Montauk Highway to Watermill, Bridgehampton, Sagaponack and Wainscott or, if you feel adventurous as I did one day, walk east across the sand for about a quarter of a mile in front of the dredge draining Mecox Bay. Carry your bike or push it across the wet sand near the waters edge to Dune Road where there is a small public rest house with outdoor picnic tables. You may then go to Sagaponack and Wainscott by back roads.

From the pavillion take Dune Road east crossing Sam's Creek. It will lead you to Job's Lane. Bear right then a sharp left at Ocean Road to the next intersection, Bridge Lane. You will turn right here and follow Bridge Lane, cross Sagaponack Lake to Sagaponack Road. Find the general store. I make it a practice to stop briefly at these out of the way stores to get the flavor of the community. At times I make a token purchase to talk to the proprietors--they are always family owned and run. It was particularly rewarding in this case. Their stock in trade was

SOUTHAMPTON
Mecox Bay
(looking north from town beach corner of Dune Rd. & Flying Pt. Rd.)

SAGAPONACK
General Store
(west side by south end of street)

varied--gas pumps outside and everything imaginable inside. Groceries, hardware, food and drinks were all obtainable. No money changed hands while I was there. Several sales were made and all sales were entered into a large ledger kept on a shelf behind the old rarely used cash register. Memories of my boyhood in rural New York flooded back to me. The gentle flow of life, the casual pace of business, the easy neighborliness were found again at Sagaponack.

Main Street crosses Montauk Highway. See the old cemetery at this corner. A left turn here will bring you back to Southampton. If you wish to continue north to Sag Harbor, as I wished that beautiful spring day continue on Sagg Road and take time to make a slight detour through Poxabogue Park, at the first left turn after you cross Montauk Highway. You can get back onto Sagg Road by turning right on the first road after you cross the railroad tracks.

SAGAPONACK
Old Cemetery
(corner of Montauk Hwy. and Main St.)

SAGAPONACK
Old Cemetery
(corner of Montauk Hwy. and Main St.)

You will ride on a sparsely travelled road. You will see modern homes and mansions, potato farms and scenery wild as nature left it.

To maintain the character of the county, an interesting program that generations unborn will appreciate has been instituted. The county will purchase the land developmental rights of farmers. The way it works is that a farmer with substantial land holding will sell his right to develop his land to the county. When the county makes the purchase that land may never be subdivided for homes but must hence forth and forever be used for agriculture or lie fallow.

Continue on Sagg Road. When you get to Sag Harbor it will change its name to Madison Street. You will see old houses, antique shops in profusion and all sorts of stores making a browsing ride most enjoyable. I stopped for coffee at

BRIDGEHAMPTON
   Poxabogue Pond Park

SAG HARBOR
   Sag Harbor Village

SAG HARBOR   *Sag Harbor Village*
(corner of Main & Madison looking southeast)

Old House on Palmer Terrace

SAG HARBOR
Custom House - First Post Office in USA

SAG HARBOR
Old Whalers Church - Steeple Was Blown Down During 1938 Storm

Inside World Famous Whaling Museum

Hilde's shop and had home made cheese cake. It and the coffee were fresh and delicious. Bike your way onto the new and spacious dock. Take a leisurely ride onto Ferry Road to North Haven and return by way of Long and Short Beach Highway; then to Main Street to see the old houses south of Palmer Terrace.

The way back to Southampton is to continue south on Main Street which will change its name to Sag Harbor Turnpike. Keep going south and turn right onto Scuttle Hole Road even though Sag Harbor Turnpike will also get you there. I chose Scuttle Hole Road to Montauk Highway because it takes you through the Scuttle Hole depression and gave me the opportunity to see a series of semi-isolated basins of kettle ponds perpendicular to the terminal moraine of the Ronkonkoma glacier that formed the south fork. Fascinating!

The return trip through Watermill and Cobb to Southampton was on heavily travelled Montauk Highway but a wide shoulder and a gentle ride by a tired biker brought me back to the town parking lot. And so ended a most beautiful bike ride and a marvelous day.

WATERMILL
    Restored Windmill
        (southside of Main St.)

WATERMILL
    Watermill Hamlet
        (northside of Main St. looking west)

    Old Mill Stone
        (southside of Main St.)

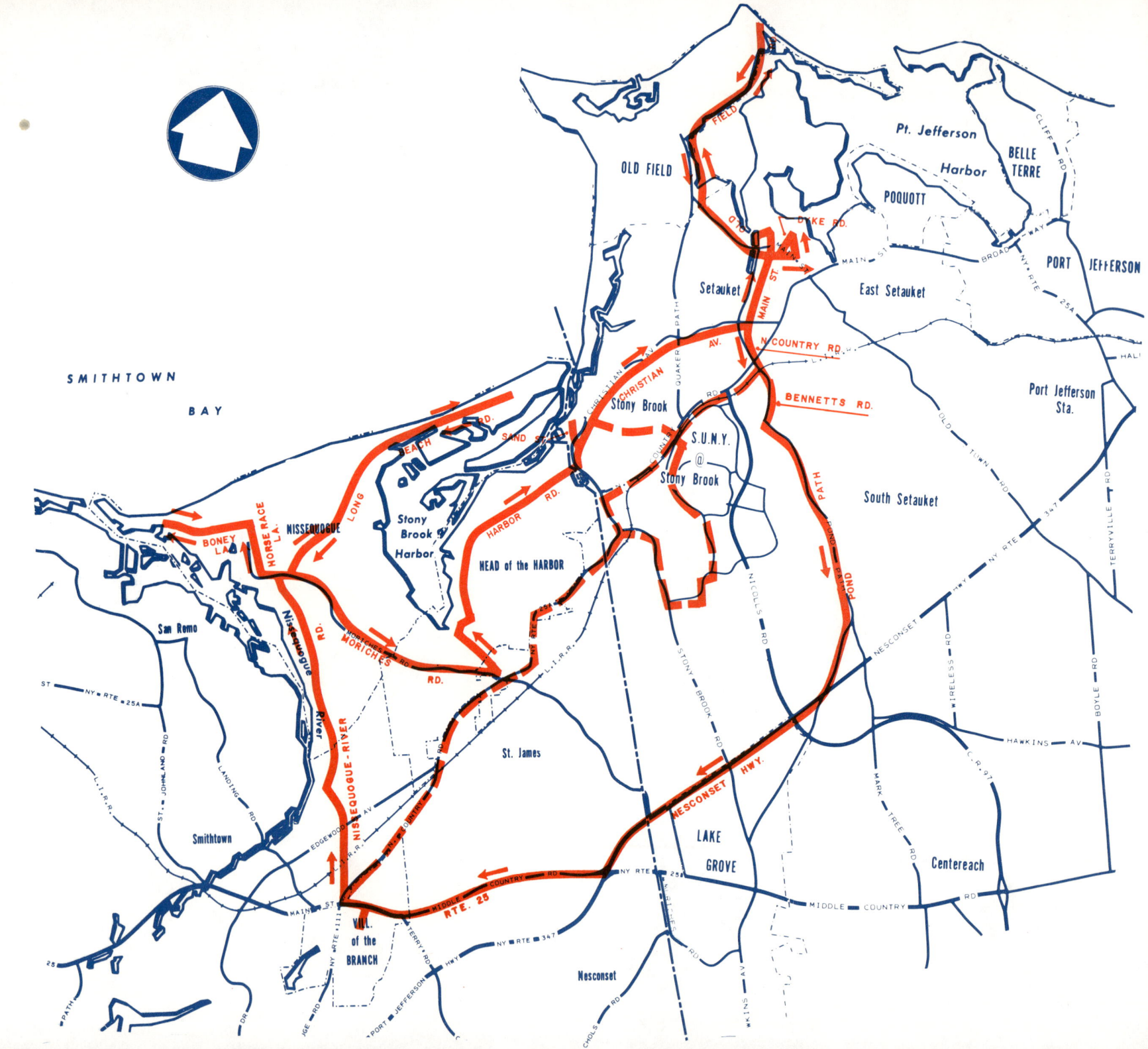

SMITHTOWN TO STONY BROOK AND SETAUKET

Park your car at the Smithtown shopping center and proceed up Nissequogue River Road. It is the road adjacent to the Presbyterian Church and is a continuation of Route 111 across Jericho Turnpike. Ride along this road for about three miles. You will glimpse the Nissequogue River on your left from time to time as you travel. The road is narrow, winding, heavily wooded and ends at Moriches Road. A brass plaque marks the homestead of Richard Smith.

If you turn to the left you will bike along Horse Race Lane to Boney Lane and after about a mile arrive at Short Beach. You will pass the Job Smith House built in the 1600's - now a private residence and not visible from the road.

A right turn on Moriches Road will take you past the original site of the Smithtown Presbyterian Church where it was built in 1675. It was dismantled and moved to its present location at

Directions

Long Island Expressway to Exit 56 North on Route 111 to Route 25 – or Northern State Parkway to its eastern extension, Smithtown By-pass to Route 111 then north to Route 25, left on 25 to The Branch Shopping Center. Park car in lot.

Distance

20 Miles.

SMITHTOWN
*Brass Plaque Homestead of R. Smith
(southside of Moriches Rd.)*

the junction of Route 25 and Nissequogue River Road in 1750. Notice the divided end section of Long Beach Road here. It goes to two of the Smithtown Beaches. This road too is hilly and winding for its two miles. The Smithtown Yacht Club and the Smithtown Marina are here in addition to the two beaches. Refreshments of sandwiches, ice cream, beer and soda are available.

The marina is in a very sheltered cove of Stony Brook Harbor; boats must navigate through Porpoise Channel on the way to and from the Sound. This channel keeps shoaling and each year is supposed to be the year of the dredge - but each year there is "an unavoidable delay". Hanging up on the sand bar has become more and more the rule rather than the exception and we all learned to sit out the ebb tide at anchor or to cruise slowly into the sunset until the tide came in. I understand that next year, surely, is the year of the dredge.

STONY BROOK
Stony Brook Harbor
(looking northwest to Porpoise Channel)

ST. JAMES
St. James General Store

To go on with the planned bike ride, return to Moriches Road and continue east. Watch out for cars hauling boats. I was almost decapitated by the wide bow of a towed boat when the driver cut in too soon after passing. You will pass 50 Acre Road (on the right). Continue to Harbor Hill Road (it will be on the left). The old General Store is at this corner - the taste of the licorice and the smell of the lavender is still with me. Opened in 1857 it is the oldest General Store on Long Island.

Turn left and coast down Harbor Hill Road. It goes north along Stony Brook Harbor with access to the Harbor in this area only at Thompson Alley, a very short distance from the bottom of the hill after the road turns right.

You will see, as you travel this not-very-busy highway, stately oaks and locust trees. They cool a hot summer day with their shade. You will see thickets of honeysuckle and smell their perfume. There will be skunk cabbage in the hollow on the southside of the road. Mountain laurel and rhododendron fill the shady areas under the dogwood trees. The thickets are full of songbirds who find the sparsely settled community very much to their liking.

Continue on Harbor Road until it ends at the Grist Mill in Stony Brook, built in 1751 and in continual operation until 1952. It is now operated in the summer as part of a Stony Brook Museum.

After passing the Grist Mill, ride to Main Street and turn left, going past the two shopping centers which fade away behind curved drives and landscaped parkland. The shops maintain the colonial architecture of the area.

Notice on the left the whaleboat and the figure head of Hercules from the U.S.S. Ohio, launched in 1820. Turn left to the Stony Brook Yacht Club (members only) and ride (carefully) along the railed promenade where people are busy fishing from dawn to dusk.

Look east from the promenade past a pair of buoys (a black and a red) and you will see the channel to the Sound that keeps getting more and more silt-laden and which will be dredged one day. I ran aground there on an outgoing tide one afternoon and waited many hours for enough water to float off. Food running out made a bad situation worse.

The shallow tidewater contains clam and oyster beds and there is good flounder fishing. Off to the right in the swifter waters bluefish and

STONY BROOK
   Grist Mill
      (corner of Harbor Rd. & Main St.)

striped bass can be caught, depending on tide, time and luck. On the spit of sand on the right are the summer homes of West Meadow Beach. I ride there in the winter and at times meet hardy souls who live there year round with only wood burning stoves to protect them from the northeast winds that rattle the shutters and lift the shingles off the roof.

STONY BROOK
Figurehead of Hercules From U.S.S. Ohio 1820

There is a small public beach at the end of the promenade with soft sand, quiet water, and a small playground for the children.

Return to Main Street. See the Three Village Inn. It has a good restaurant, a full menu, a good bar and fine service. Prices are moderate. Rooms at the Inn are $35.00 for a double and the cottages facing the Marina are a little higher: $40.00 for a double. Make your reservations months in advance.

The Museums and sightseeing in Stony Brook could take a good part of the day or many days; a pamphlet entitled "Heritage Walk" can be obtained at the cashier's desk at the Inn.

Bike past the Three Village Inn to Main Street and continue east. It changes its name to Christian Avenue. If you decide to end the trip here you can return to Smithtown by turning right onto Hollow Road and riding to its end at Cedar Street. Turn right on Cedar Street to 25A. (Stony Brook Station). At this point you can turn right on 25A and bicycle back to Smithtown where your car is parked, or you can choose a return trip through Stony Brook University.

STONY BROOK
Three Village Inn

If you choose the University Route, turn left for about 100 feet on 25A to the Railroad Station; you will take the foot path that crosses the tracks to the University road. Turn right on this road. A bike path parallels the road on the right, but it is interrupted from time to time and you may prefer to stay on the main road since traffic is very light. Keep bearing right, heading for parking lot P or South Campus. Beyond the parking lot you will find Stony Brook Road. Turn right on it to 25A and left on 25A to Smithtown.

Those of you who wish to go on to historic Setauket, continue on Christian Avenue to its end, Main Street.

STONY BROOK
S.U.N.Y. At Stony Brook

STONY BROOK
Carriage House Museum

A thrilling and historically truthful tale of espionage during the American Revolution is told by Corey Ford in his book, "A Peculiar Service". Patriots from Setauket played a leading role in America's first intelligence corps. "They kept General Washington supplied with a steady flow of military intelligence and succeeded in outwitting British counter intelligence to the end of the Revolution." George Smith, a lineal descendant of Richard Smith, in 1781 volunteered to serve as an intelligence gatherer, or spy, for the Culper ring (the code name for George Washington's secret service). At great risk he forwarded vital information needed by Washington on the movements of General Clinton's troops on Long Island. This was done while Setauket was occupied by the British.

19

At Main Street, turn left to the Village Green. You will pass the Setauket Post Office. Just beyond is the Presbyterian Church, built in 1812. The previous church on that site was used by the British as a barracks during the Revolution. Slightly to the west is the Caroline Episcopal Church, built in 1729. Spend some time biking through this area. You will find the bike path around the Frank Melville Memorial Park (next to the Post Office) interesting.

Notice the stone mill. This was built in 1937 as part of the Memorial Park. Walk or bike along the path that winds gently and pleasantly under a cover of trees and skirts the edge of Setauket Harbor. The mountain laurel and rhododendron grow in profusion. There are grassy open spots that invite sitting.

SETAUKET
Presbyterian Church
(corner of Dyke Rd. & Main St.)

SETAUKET
Post Office
(northside of Main St.)

Retrace your path on Main Street past Christian Avenue to the other end of Setauket. A very well restored home, the Thompson House built in 1700, is worth visiting. Admission is $1.00. The rooms have authentic colonial home-made furnishings and the guided tour is memorable. The offices of the Society for the Preservation of Long Island Antiquities are in an old house next to the Thompson House. There are shops and stores in this area. If time permits, take a pleasant bike ride through the quiet roads of Strong's Neck which projects into Port Jefferson Harbor like a tilted mushroom.

For the strong of heart and limb, there is an additional ride along Old Field Road to its end at Old Field Point Lighthouse. The lighthouse is closed to the public but the road nearby presents a spectacular view of the Sound and distant Connecticut.

Emma S. Clark Library

SETAUKET

Grist Mill At Ward Melville Park

Thompson House

SETAUKET

Mill Pond At Ward Melville Park

STONY BROOK
Town Beach (Shore Rd. & Sand St.)

OLD FIELD
Old Field Point Lighthouse

STONY BROOK
Shopping Center and Post Office

The return to your car in Smithtown can be made in several ways. The way I prefer is to take North Country Road south from the Thompson House across 25A. Here its name changes to Bennett's Road. It dead ends at Sheep Pasture Road where you turn left. Continue to the first fork in the road. You take the right one, Pond Path. Continue on Pond Path until it intersects Route 347 (Nesconset Highway). Turn to the right

SETAUKET
Caroline Episcopal Church

STONY BROOK
Stony Brook Harbor

continue until it crosses Route 25, Jericho Turnpike. Both these roads are heavily travelled but have good wide shoulders and are fairly level. At Route 25 turn right and you will be at your car in 10 minutes.

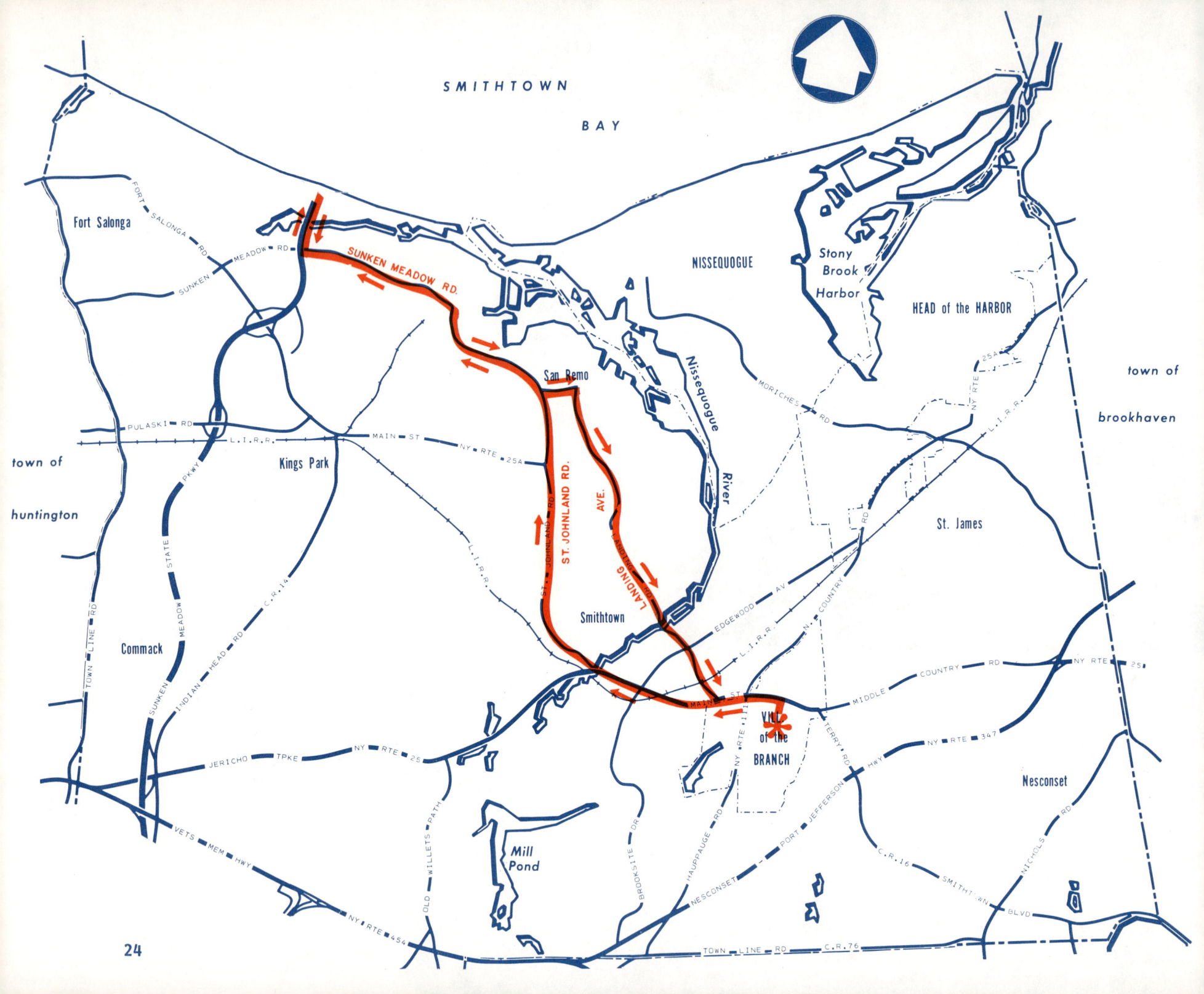

SMITHTOWN

Directions

Long Island Expressway to Exit 56 North on N.Y. Route 111 to N.Y. Route 25 - or Northern State Parkway to its eastern extension, Veterans Memorial Hwy. - Nesconset Hwy. (N.Y. Rte. 347) to Route 111 then north to N.Y. Route 25.

Distance

8 Miles

It is recorded that in 1650, one Edmond Wood and partners purchased from the Nessaquake Indians land east of the Nissequogue River to Stony Brook. The southern boundary was the Connetequot River and it extended on the west to Huntington. This area, now the Town of Smithtown, was purchased from the Indians for 6 coats, 6 fathoms of wampum, 6 hoes, 6 hatchets, 6 knives, 6 kettles and 100 muxes (steel drills used in the manufacture of wampum) all to be paid by the 29th of September 1650.

One account of this transaction says that Mr. Wood and partners failed to record this perfectly legal purchase with the proper authorities while another account states that the sale was recorded but that the requirement that the land be settled and used was not fulfilled. Be that as it may, the land reverted to the Indians.

The legend that Richard "Bull" Smith purchased this land from the Indians and that the boundaries were determined by the area he could circumnavigate on the back of a bull in one day is interesting, but it is a story that Mr. Richard Smythe would not have accepted very kindly. (In the 17th century, the "i" and "y" were used interchangeably). He had been a soldier in Cromwell's Army, was the son of an army officer, a member of the landowning class, and a gentleman. It is possible that the legend had its basis in the fact that the Smith family crest has a half-bull rampant on the top of its shield.

Richard Smith sailed from Yorkshire, England on October 2, 1635, and landed in Boston where he stayed briefly. From there he sailed to Southampton and became active in town affairs. His 15 year residence was interrupted by a short visit to England. When he returned to Massachusetts Bay he and eight other Quakers aboard were promptly arrested but were soon released. He returned to Southampton where the Puritan residents too feared contamination of their Puritanism by the apostate to the Quaker faith. He was given a week to depart; therefore he and his friends left for Setauket which was then being settled.

The Montauk Indians claimed all of Long Island from Canarsie Bay to Montauk Point. It was at Richard Smith's home in Setauket in 1659 that Lion Gardiner received a gift of land from the Grand Sachem of the Montauks. That land comprises the Town of Smithtown and Gardiner's Island, which is still in the possession of his descendants.

The reason for this magnanimous gift was to reward Mr. Gardiner for the part he played in the return of the Sachem's daughter after her capture by the Narraganset Indians during one of their periodic raids on Long Island. Mr. Gardiner had interests in Connecticut and in Long Island and maintained friendly relations with the Indians on both sides of the Sound.

Richard Smith was a witness to the deed transferring this land to Mr. Gardiner and signed it. Four years later, he either purchased the Smithtown area from Lion Gardiner or received it as a bequest in his will. To establish firm legal claim, he sought for and received a patent from Governor Nicholls in 1665 and another in 1677 (the Andros Patent). He immediately proceeded to settle his wife and 9 children on his land; he surveyed it and established its boundaries.

You will travel some of the old areas of Smithtown on your bicycle. You will see some 17th century and 18th century remains of our colonial heritage and you will ride winding, narrow, hilly roads canopied with oaks. Dogwood will be in bloom in early May and there will be mountain laurel flowering in profusion in early June. Most of the area is sparsely settled and wild honeysuckle is permitted free rein. It perfumes the countryside.

Street park your car on Plaza Drive. It is a small road that butts into Main Street about 1000 feet east of the intersection of Routes 111 and 25. Mount your bicycle and cross the highway. Almost directly across from Plaza Drive is Epenetus Smith's Tavern, Number 209 east Main Street. It was a stopping place for the Brooklyn - Sag Harbor Stage Coach. Nearby was the Blydenburgh House where Washington "baited his horses" on a trip through Long Island. Travel west and turn the corner at the library and see the Caleb Smith House adjacent to the library parking lot. It was built in 1819 and is now the home of the Smithtown Historical Society. It was moved here from Commack. Across the street is an old cemetery where many of the Smiths and Blydenburghs are buried. On the west corner across from the cemetery is the beautiful old Presbyterian Church. It was built in 1675, not at this site but at the headwaters of the Nissequogue River where Richard Smith built his home and where the original town began.

SMITHTOWN
Epenetus Smith Tavern
(E. Main St.)

SMITHTOWN
    Plaque At Smithtown Library

Smithtown Public Library

SMITHTOWN

Old Cemetery
    (across from Library)

The Church remained there for 75 years, then in 1750 was dismantled and moved to its present location on land donated by Obadiah and Epenetus Smith, grandsons of Richard Smith.

During those 75 years additional areas of land at the headwaters of the Nissequogue River were developed and the rich farmland of the interior was cultivated. Access to these lands was by barges and lighters floating up the River on

27

SMITHTOWN
First Presbyterian Church
(Main St.)

an incoming tide with cargos transferred from ships that anchored in the deep water of the Sound at the mouth of the River or that were tied up at the "Lower Docks" which had been built at Old Dock Road, now Kings Park. The barges and lighters floated to the "Upper Docks" at Landing Avenue where a narrow bridge now spans the river.

Across Main Street from the Presbyterian Church next to the shopping center parking lot is Singer Lane. Number 9, a small building now a gift shop, was Smithtown's first schoolhouse where Walt Whitman taught briefly in 1837.

Continue west on Main Street to Edgewater Avenue on the left. Its continuation is New Mill Road and leads to Blydenburgh Park. You can see a mill there that was built by Caleb and Joshua Smith and Isaac Blydenburgh. It is enclosed by wire mesh fencing and is in a sad state of disrepair. It is hardly worth making the trip since we will visit another very well preserved grist mill elsewhere in the Smithtown area.

SMITHTOWN
Smithtown's First School House
(east side Singer La.)

28

Continue west on the southside of Route 25. Use the sidewalk, go down the hill and cross the rustic bridge over the Nissequogue River that parallels the Main Highway. There is a vest-pocket park and a comfortable bench on the river bank. Cross the street to the statue of the bull inscribed to commemorate the founding of Smithtown by Richard Smith, "The Bull Rider", in 1665.

SMITHTOWN
Smithtown Bull

Continue west on 25A for about two miles (it has a nice wide shoulder and is comfortable to ride upon) to where 25A makes a sharp turn to the left. Do not make this left turn but continue straight on - the name changes to St. Johnland Road. About one mile along St. Johnland Road, on the right, you will find the Obediah Smith House built in 1700. It has been beautifully restored by the Smithtown Historical Society. Even the brick oven, designed to be fired and loaded from inside the house, is in good shape. It was built into a hill, and a stone fence creates a walkway around the northside. Two ramps, one covered, give access to the second floor from this side. The main entrance is on the southside into the ground floor. It is open to the public, but make arrangements through the Smithtown Historical Society since I have never found it open on any of my trips.

You may at this point, if the weather is hot, decide to continue traveling west for about a mile and visit Sunken Meadow State Park with its fine sandy beach and other recreational facilities. A snack bar serving beer, coffee and sandwiches, is open daily from 10-4 weekdays and 9-4 weekends. If you decide to continue bicycling through Smithtown, you must retrace your path along St. Johnland Road and continue about 1/2 mile east to Landing Road. It is the first traffic light after the Obediah Smith House.

Turn left onto Landing Road. It makes a curve to the right and here its name changes to Landing Avenue. A short distance along Landing Avenue you will find the Smithtown Landing Country Club open to the public except for its swimming pool which is open to members only. The bar has everything and the beer is very cold. You may not wet your outside in the pool, but they have everything needed to wet your inside. Lunches and dinners are served and the place is immaculate. Lunches range from $2.95 and dinners from $5.95. You may wish to tour the Country

KINGS PARK

Obadiah Smith House
(northside of St. Johnlands Rd.)

Obadiah Smith House

SMITHTOWN
Nissequogue River (looking northwest)

Club and enjoy the view of the mouth of the Nissequogue River with its beautiful mud flats in the winter which turn into tall stands of thatch in the summer.

Continue south on Landing Avenue after you leave the Country Club grounds and you will see on the left the Methodist Church, built in 1834. Further south is a narrow bridge. This is the upper dock area of old Smithtown. The barges and the lighters floated here to unload their cargo of fertilizer and manufactured goods taking on shipments of wood and farm products for New York City and New England.

Continue over the bridge – up the short hill, which I must walk, and on to Main Street, 1/4 mile ahead to where your car is parked.

Sunken Meadow State Park
(prom. overlook by 3 mile marker looking west)

KINGS PARK
Sunken Meadow State Park
(bathhouse entrance)

Smithtown Methodist Church - 1834
(eastside Landing Ave.)

SMITHTOWN

Landing Ave. Park
(eastside Landing Ave.)

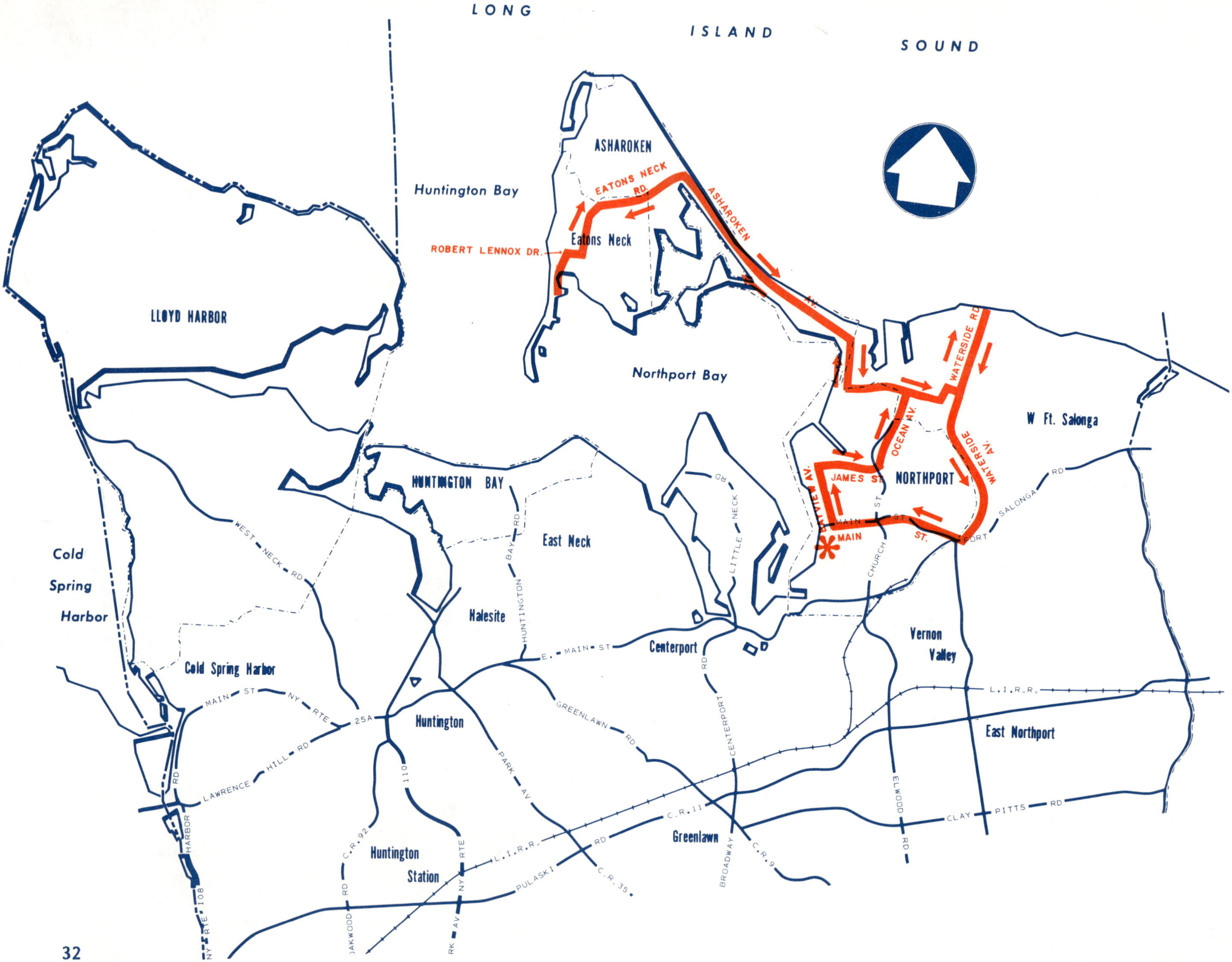

LONG ISLAND SOUND
Huntington Bay
ASHAROKEN
EATONS NECK RD.
ASHAROKEN AV.
ROBERT LENNOX DR.
Eatons Neck
LLOYD HARBOR
Northport Bay
WATERSIDE RD
OCEAN AV.
WATERSIDE AV.
W Ft. Salonga
JAMES ST.
NORTHPORT
BAYVIEW AV.
MAIN ST.
MAIN ST.
FORT SALONGA RD
CHURCH ST
HUNTINGTON BAY
East Neck
LITTLE NECK RD
Cold Spring Harbor
WEST NECK RD
Halesite
HUNTINGTON BAY RD
E. MAIN ST
Centerport
Vernon Valley
Cold Spring Harbor
MAIN ST
NY RTE 25A
Huntington
GREENLAWN RD
CENTERPORT RD
L.I.R.R.
East Northport
LAWRENCE HILL RD
PARK AV
110
ELWOOD RD
CLAY PITTS RD
HARBOR RD
C.R. 11
Greenlawn
C.R. 92
Huntington Station
NY RTE
L.I.R.R.
RD
C.R. 9
BROADWAY
C.R. 35
PULASKI RD
OAKWOOD RD
PARK AV
NY RTE 108

NORTHPORT -

ASHAROKEN BEACH - EATONS NECK

Directions

Northern State Parkway - Exit 42. Take N.Y. Route 231, North, to Jericho Turnpike (N.Y. Rte. 25). Right on Route 25 to Elwood Road - Left on Elwood Road to Main Street Northport. Left on Main Street to end.

Distance

15 Miles (Bicycle)

Park your car at the Town Parking Lot at the foot of Main Street. Take time to ride around this beautiful town that has remained more or less unchanged for the last 40 years. I remember it basically as it is when I saw it for the first time in 1936. It was there that I met my wife and courted her - and visited her at her summer place on a high hill near where 25A makes its sharp turn to run parallel with Northport harbor. Walk out on the fishing dock and notice that the harbor seems to be completely land-locked, that it resembles a large lake rather than a snug refuge from the storms that blow up on the Sound. But woe to the sailor or pleasure boat skipper who disregards, or misses the buoys that mark the tortuous channel from the Sound into this haven. Many a propellor has been lost, many a shaft has been bent, and many a boat has been grounded through carelessness or through ignorance in boat handling.

The harbors of the North Shore owe their origin to three natural causes in early geological times. There was the action of under glacial springs converting sand to quicksand so that large masses of the North Shore bluffs flowed into the sea. Secondly, there was erosion by subglacial springs; and thirdly, the harbors were plowed out by projecting spurs of ice from the glaciers. The adjacent elevations are due to the ice that thrust out on the sides.

But, I am a little ahead of the story. Long Island owes its topography to glacial action during the periods of the Ice Ages. The glaciers flowing from the northwest stopped near the center of the Island - viewed from north to south. They left two morrainal ridges that traverse the Island from east to west. The northern ridge, the Harbor Hill moraine, proceedes in a north easterly direction from Gravesend Bay to Orient Point reaching a height of 390 feet and forms the north fork. The southern ridge, the Ronkonkoma Moraine, goes from Manhattan eastward and ends at

Montauk Point forming Long Islands southfork. The two morainal ridges cross south of Manhasset and reach the highest point, 410 feet, at High Hill, south of Huntington. Between these two ridges are areas of sand and gravel with depressions, hills, plains, valleys and plateaus. South of the southern ridge, the outward plain of fine sand and gravel stretches to the sea.

On the first day of spring, my bike and I walked the fishing dock at Northport. The scene was bucolic. There were the serious fishermen with two rods -- and there were the laughing happy ones. One girl lay full out on her back on a 12" beam; her rod lay diagonally across her body, her radio was turned on softly and she welcomed the sun. There were mothers walking their children, there were groups talking and there were of course some engrossed in books enjoying the early spring.

NORTHPORT
Northport Village Park
(west end of Main St.)

NORTHPORT
Northport Village
(looking east up Main St.)

After this walk, mount your bike and ride along Bayview Avenue. It is the street adjacent to the park. Make a right turn onto James Street, then turn left onto Ocean Avenue. (You can see Asharoken Beach in the distance almost bisecting Northport Harbor.) To the right are the four stacks of the Long Island Lighting Company, Northport Plant. On the left, a housing development that is not in an excavation of glacial origin, but was built in an abandoned sandpit. Now turn left onto Eaton's Neck Road and ride through Asharoken Beach.

This isthmus connecting Northport and Eaton's Neck has Northport Harbor on the one side and Long Island Sound on the other. Ride slowly along this road and enjoy the view. On a clear day the area around Stamford Connecticut can be

NORTHPORT
Asharoken Beach
  (on James St. looking northwest)
LILCO Northport Plant
  (looking southeast from Asharoken Beach)

NORTHPORT
New Housing Development in Sand Pit
  (looking down from James St.)
Stamford, Conn.
  (looking north from James St.)

seen clearly. You will notice, about a mile out on the Sound, a barge-like float with a long, slender superstructure. It is a tie-up for tankers which couple their hoses to underwater conduits to empty their oil into the LILCO storage tanks.

Continue on Eaton's Neck Road towards West beach. You will pass a road leading to Eaton's Neck Lighthouse. It is a beautiful sight from the water, but unfortunately there is a "Do Not Enter" sign on the road to it. It might be fun to explore but it is not advisable without permission. Take a tour through the Eaton's Neck residential community. Then turn right on Robert Lennox Drive to the beach. Make your way on foot through West Beach to the end of the Peninsula. It is beautiful and solitary.

EATONS NECK
*Eatons Neck Coast Guard Station
(north end of Lighthouse Rd.)*

EATONS NECK
West Beach

You can walk down the Peninsula on the Sound side and return along the bay shore. The Village of Huntington Bay and Little Neck are directly across the channel to Northport Bay. Keep close to the waters edge as you walk since the entire area is a bird sanctuary. The nesting birds protest loudly at human intrusion but no harm is done if you keep close to the shore line and keep out of nesting areas. Signs along the beach prohibit landing of boats.

To return to Northport, go back by Eaton's Neck Road but do not turn right at Ocean Avenue but continue ahead to Waterside Road, where Eaton's Neck Road ends. You can turn right here and return to Northport or you can turn left and take a side trip to Crab Meadow Beach 1/2 mile away. It is the gathering place for the high school boys and girls who flock there by jeep, truck, jalopy, sports car and bike.

NORTHPORT
Crab Meadow Golf Course
(northeast end of Seaside Ct.)

"How do you get the first empty bottle?" We mailed him a half-dozen empties. He had a terrible time at the Argentina Customs explaining those empty Coke bottles. They were positive that some nefarious plot that they could not fathom was in the making. Customs finally surrendered them, still positive that somehow they had been "had".

Return along Waterside to where it joins Route 25A and Main Street. Turn right on Main Street, continue to the end, and you will find your car where you left it at the dock. If it is not too late, visit a small park and playground about 400 feet south of the waterfront parking lot. There are comfortable benches facing the bay and happy children to watch. No food is available at either Eaton's Neck or Asharoken beach but you can eat at a Diner on Main Street, Northport, just a few yards east of the dock, on

NORTHPORT
Crab Meadow Beach
(north end of Waterside Rd.)

On this first day of spring, when I was there, the air was balmy, school was out, and so were the kids. The radios and tapes were blaring, the frisbees were scooting, and there was a feeling of happiness that said all was right with the world. The typical beach pavilions were in good shape - the outdoor charcoal cookers were intact - only the ubiquitous glass from broken bottles was all over the parking lot. Our legislators should require that all containers be recycled, particularly bottles.

Argentina has had this law for many years and is very strict about it. A very good friend went to live in Buenos Aires. In a letter to us he mentioned a "Catch 22" dilemma. He and his family loved Coke but no storekeeper in Buenos Aires will sell you a bottle of Coke to take home unless you give him an empty bottle. He wrote,

NORTHPORT
Northport Village Museum
(Main St.)

Northport Village

NORTHPORT
Cow Harbor Park
(westside Woodbine Ave.)

Cow Harbor Park
(westside Woodbine Ave.)

NORTHPORT
    Mariner's Inn
    (west end of James St.)

NORTHPORT
    Mariner's Inn
    (west end of James St.)

Feed & Grain Restaurant
(northside Main St.)

the southside. I have known it for 40 years; it is clean and has good home cooked food or you might want to try the Northport Feed and Grain Restaurant a bit further east on the northside of the street - a bit tea-roomy, but good. For those who wish to luxuriate and have a beautiful view of the harbor while dining, there is the Mariner's Inn. It is at the top of the hill, on Bayview Avenue. This is the street that runs north behind the town parking lot. On many occasions I have tied my boat up at the Mariner's Inn private dock, had lunch, then sailed home with a feeling of a day well spent.

39

40

CAUMSETT STATE PARK

Directions

Northern State Parkway to N.Y. Route 110. North. Exit 40 - Route 110 to Main Street, Huntington - Left on Main Street (N.Y. Rte. 25A) to West Neck Road

Distance

10 miles.

In 1677 James Lloyd of Boston purchased the parts of Caumsett that were owned by a Thomas Hart. Since he had, by this purchase, become the Lord of the Manor, he renamed it Lloyd's Neck and it remained in the Lloyd family for 200 years.

In 1926 Marshall Field III purchased 1,750 acres of Lloyd's Neck and made it into a large estate which he renamed "Caumsett" - the old Indian name for the area. This wasteland, by dint of much effort and with a spare-no-expense determination, was metamorphosed into an English Manor with tennis, riding and polo, pheasant and skeet shooting, and trout fishing. He built a beautiful beach and a deep-water dock for his yacht "Coursande". To get around the estate and knit the facilities together, he built 25 miles of road. In addition to the mansion, there were a summer cottage, a winter cottage, a dairy farm and polo pony barns, as well as 20 cottages for the 85 employees who were needed to help run the estate.

LLOYD HARBOR
Entrance to Caumsett State Park

In 1961 the State of New York bought Caumsett from the Marshall Field Foundation, and from Mrs. Ruth Pruyer Field, for $4,275,000. Marshall Field's will dictated that the future use of the Estate shall be "for environmental purposes stressing natural observation and beauty found at Caumsett." The Board of Cooperative Education of Nassau County is currently using the Summer House and plans to increase the scope of its outdoor and Environmental Educational Program by including the Big Stone House in its plans for future expanded programs. The Mansion has been used intermittently for community programs, but Queens College will be using it for courses in Environmental Technology as soon as alterations are completed.

LLOYD HARBOR

James Lloyd Manor House

LLOYD HARBOR

Henry Lloyd House

At the south eastern end of the Estate adjacent to a brickwall with an arched entryway is the Henry Lloyd House, built in 1711. It is a small yellow building now being restored by the Huntington Historical Society. The restoration will include an apartment for a rentor or a caretaker since it has been found that use of public buildings by private or public rentors serves to preserve the buildings and keep vandalism to a minimum. It is interesting to note that Jupiter Hammon, a slave of the Lloyd family lived in this house and was the first black poet in America to have his work published. It is known that his remains are buried somewhere near but searches for the grave have been unsuccessful.

You will find at Caumsett many miles of road that can be ridden on a bike. Detailed maps are distributed at the security gate. Since autos, except for maintenance vehicles, are prohibited, one can ride at leisure, 2 or 3 abreast, and enjoy the open areas, the woodlands and the beach. For the intrepid bike rider, there are miles of unimproved roads through and along the marsh, along the edge of Long Island Sound, and around the beach. At times you will have to walk where the road has been filled in with sand or where it has deteriorated.

Since the entire park is a bird sanctuary, the silent bike rider can have a veritable field day - searching for and viewing bird life. Many ornithological groups use the facilities in the warmer months.

LLOYD HARBOR
  Lloyd Harbor
  (looking east from West Neck Rd.)

LLOYD HARBOR
  Bicycle Path to Lloyd Harbor
  (westside West Neck Rd.)

To get to the park, drive to Huntington. A few blocks west of Route 110, on the right, Main Street intersects West Neck Road. Notice a bicycle path on the west side of the street. After about three miles the road runs along a narrow isthmus with Cold Spring Harbor and Cove Neck on your left (west) and Lloyd Harbor on your right (east). When the road turns sharply to the right and runs along the shore of Lloyd Harbor, it changes its name to Lloyd Harbor Road. The entrance to Caumsett Park is about a mile east on the left.

There is adequate parking at Caumsett Park, but if you plan to spend the day, be sure to bring lunch along, since no food or drinks can be bought. I found that an interesting and exciting day can be spent by parking the car at the Caumsett Park lot, spending two or three hours at the park, then biking to Target Rock Wildlife Refuge, an 80-acre National Park about two miles east of Caumsett off Lloyd Harbor Road. Ride past the Dead End sign and you will see the road to the park on the right.

This wildlife refuge was opened in 1970 for limited public use for nature study, photography and hiking. The trails lead through a forest, a pond, and to a beach at Huntington Harbor and the Sound. Bicycles must be locked at the parking lot and the trails must be walked.

Permits must be obtained for use of the park. Large parties must make prior arrangements - Small parties (four or less) can on weekdays, get their permits at the main house on arrival. If the trip is planned for a weekend, it is advisable to phone on Friday and a permit will be left with the gate-keeper. Phone (516) 271-2409. The park is open all year from 9:00 A.M.--5:00 P.M.

LLOYD HARBOR
Entrance to Target Rock Wildlife Refuge

LLOYD HARBOR
Target Rock Wildlife Refuge

You can bike or drive to Huntington or Cold Spring Harbor for lunch, returning to the park by an alternate route. Turn on West Neck Road and you can go back by the route you followed, on the bicycle path almost all the way through a sparsely settled, very attractive residential community which leads you to Huntington; or you can turn right when you get to Middle Hollow Road. Make a left turn at Jennings Road (Middle Hollow Road ends there) and continue to the second road on the right, Goose Hill Road. This will take you to Main Street - Cold Spring Harbor. Here you can go east to Huntington or west to the Village of Cold Spring Harbor.

Eating places in both Huntington and Cold Spring Harbor are discussed in the chapters devoted to those areas.

LLOYD HARBOR
 Lloyd Harbor
  (looking east from West Neck Rd.)

LLOYD HARBOR
 Target Rock Park

46

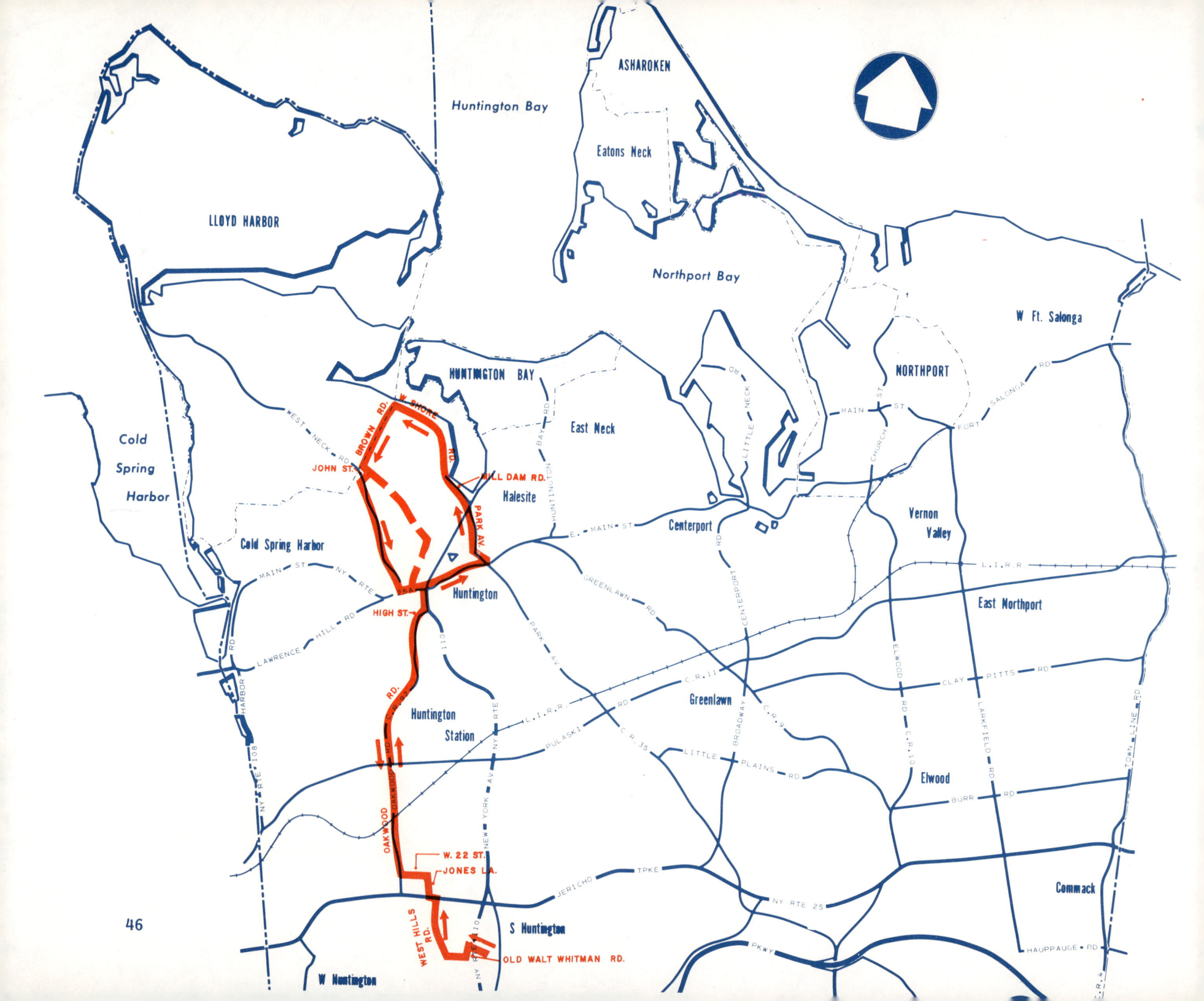

HUNTINGTON -
HISTORIC SITES AND
PRE - REVOLUTIONARY HOUSE

The first old house on today's trip is the Whitman homestead built by the poet's father on Whitman Road across Route 110, is of hand fashioned beams held together by wooden pegs and is open to the public on Wednesday, Thursday and Friday from 1:00 P.M. - 4:00 P.M. from 10:00 A.M. - 4:00 P.M. and on Saturdays and Sundays. From the Whitman House, cross the street and turn right to the first corner, West Hills Road. Within a mile you will see four pre-revolutionary houses, all private residences and not open to the public. First, the Whitman-Rome House built in 1705 on Chichester Road a bit to the left of West Hills Road, then the Joseph Whitman House, built before 1692. The third, the Whitman-Carll House built in 1780 and finally the Whitman-White House built in 1692.

Directions

Northern State Parkway or Long Island Expressway. Exit N.Y. Route 110 - go north to Walt Whitman Shopping Center on Route 110. Park your car at the south end of the shopping center near the theatre.

HUNTINGTON
Walt Whitman House

HUNTINGTON
Memorial Stone at Walt Whitman House

HUNTINGTON
Peace and Plenty Inn

Continue north on West Hills Road, cross Jericho Turnpike and turn left to the next corner, Jones Road. Turn right on Jones Road to West 22nd Street and turn left here to Oakwood Road. Turn right on Oakwood Road for 2.5 miles to High Street. At number 2 High Street you can visit the Conklin House, built in 1700. It is open Tuesday through Friday and Sunday 1:00 P.M. - 4:00 P.M. Admission, including a tour of another old building, the Jarvis House, is $1.50.

Bike to Main Street by turning left on New York Avenue and go east (right) on Main. In a short time you will pass a marble column, a memorial to Nathan Hale who visited Huntington twice during the Revolutionary War. The first trip in May of 1776, was to lead an expedition that attempted the capture of the ringleaders of loyalist groups who were supplying English warships stationed in Long Island Sound. He was in the uniform of a Captain of the Continental army

HUNTINGTON
Conklin House
(High St.)

48

took four days to make his way to Norwalk, Connecticut and from there he embarked on a trip across the Sound to Huntington Harbor--now firmly in British control. He was captured with incriminating documents and hanged as a spy the next morning, September 22, 1776, at the age of 21.

This bike ride will take you to the shore of Huntington Harbor where you will see a rock commemorating the landing of Captain Nathan Hale.

Continue riding on Main Street, pass the Soldiers and Sailors Memorial Building and the Old Town Burying Ground that was desecrated by the British to build Fort Golgotha on the top of the hill. The tombstones were used for breastworks as were the timbers of the Old First Church across the street from the Burying Ground. A new Old First Church was built on the same site after the war.

HUNTINGTON
: *Old Town Hall*
: *(northside Main St.)*

HUNTINGTON
: *Nathan Hale Memorial*
: *(Main St.)*

then. The second visit was as a spy for General Washington. He landed on the shore of Huntington Bay in the dead of night with his Yale College diploma in his knapsack, claiming to be a teacher of Latin displaced by the war. His assignment was to gather information on British troop strength and movements.

With the defeat of the Continental Army at the Battle of Long Island (Brooklyn), General Washington, with his headquarters on Manhattan Island, needed to know as much as possible of General Howe's plans. Captain Nathan Hale volunteered to attempt to gather this information. He

The Huntington Common starts at Sabbath Path on the left and extends east on both sides of Main Street. The brass plaque says that "Thomas Weeks in 1739 sold three acres and 80 rods to his seven neighbors to be used as a commons and to lie open and common forever." He got 1 pound 16 shillings for it.

Bike east on Main Street to the next Intersection, Park Avenue, where you will see a small red building. It is called the Arsenal-- built in 1748 and used by the Colonial Militia for the storage of muskets and gunpowder before the British occupation in September of 1776. It is open to the public on Sundays only 1:00 P.M. - 4:00 P.M.

HUNTINGTON
Old First Church (northside Main St.)

*Soldiers & Sailors Memorial Building
(southside Main St.)*

HUNTINGTON

*Old Town Burying Grounds
(southside Main St.)*

Heckscher Park Art Museum

HUNTINGTON

Heckscher Park Theater

Brass Plaque on Village Green

HUNTINGTON

Brass Plaque on Village Green

Brass Plaque on Village Green

HUNTINGTON

*Huntington Commons
(looking southwest to Park Ave.)*

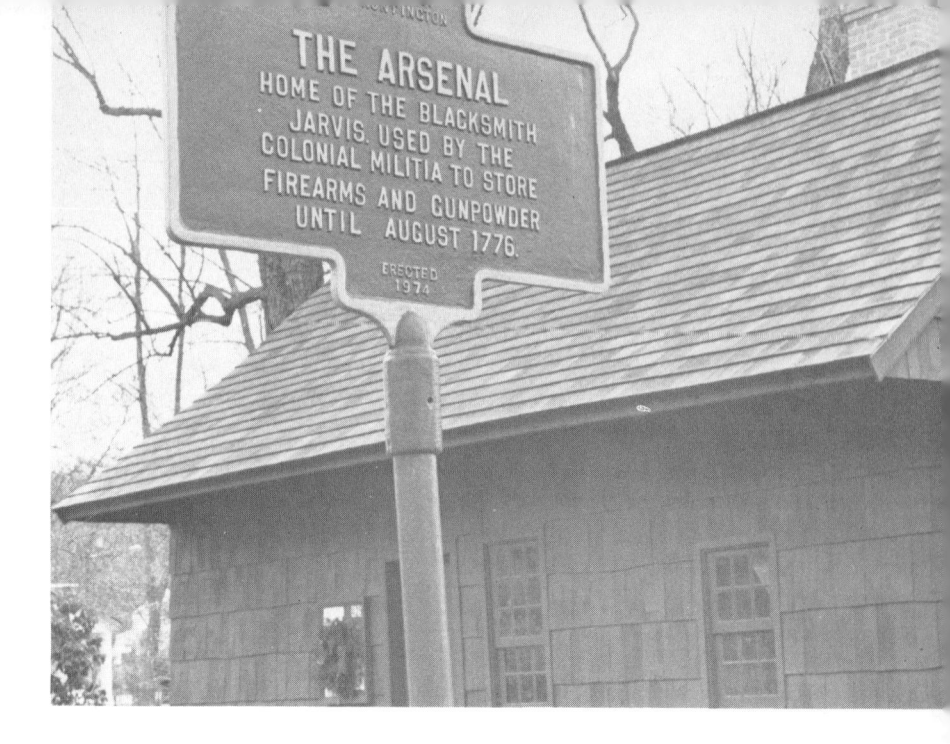

HUNTINGTON

*The Arsenal
(westside of Park Ave.)*

    Across the street is the Powell-Jarvis House built in 1795. The wing to the right is part of the original construction and served as a kitchen unitl 1841 when it was converted into a formal dining room. Further changes in the 1920's raised the wing to its present two story height. The barn behind the house was built in 1787 at Lloyd's Harbor and moved to its present site in 1972. It is a museum now.

    Next door is the Jarvis-Fleet House. The small wing is the original house, built in 1653. The large "addition" was built by Whaling Captain William Jarvis in 1702.

    Continue north on Park Avenue. You will pass the Huntington Hospital and at 244 Park Avenue notice the house with the small "eyebrow win-

HUNTINGTON
  Powell-Jarvis House
  (eastside of Park Ave.)

244 Park Avenue

HUNTINGTON
  Nathan Hale Memorial Rock
  (corner of Mill Dam Rd. & New York Ave.)

dows" above the ground floor, making the house one and one-half stories high. The windows are also called "tummy windows", since it is necessary to lie on the floor to see out. A little beyond this house, on the same side of Park Avenue, is an artfully made stone wall. Each sea and wave-polished rock was set carefully into wet mortar. The house was built about 1850 and the wall about 1890.

At the end of Park Avenue and at the intersection of New York Avenue and Mill Dam Road you will see another remembrance of Nathan Hale, the Memorial Rock placed at the shore of Huntington Bay at the spot where Captain Hale was believed to have landed on his spy mission for General Washington. Three bronze plaques tell the story of his heroic exploit.

Mill Dam Road will take you along the busy waterfront with its marinas, boat yards and beaches to West Shore Road. Turn right on West Shore Road along the south shore of Huntington Bay to Browns Road. You will see a Norman castle, occupied now by the Universalist Unitarian Fellowship. To the north, at the water's edge, is a second and smaller castle that can be reached by a road going downhill, beyond the entrance to the Eagle Hill School. The Norman castle boat house, with its steeply pitched red roof, its tall red brick capped chimneys and its buttressed walls, has its windows and doors sealed with cement blocks. This is to foil vandals who took their toll in the destruction of several small accessory houses. A sea wall of quarried granite blocks and a wide dock extending into the harbor give evidence of active use in prior years. Up hill from the boat house is the grand main castle. It is occupied by the Eagle Hill School now and its grand Norman style is set a bit askew by a very modern flat roofed tan and white brick addition at one end of the red brick soaring castle.

The story is told that a Mr. McKesson took his new bride on the "Grand Tour" of Europe at the beginning of this century. She said that she would like a Norman castle on the shore of Huntington Bay. He must have loved her dearly for he built her three of them. The large one on the hill for them to live in, the one on Browns Road occupied by the Universalist Unitarian Fellowship was for the help, and the third and smallest is the boat house.

HUNTINGTON
Norman Castle
(now Universalist Unitarian Fellowship Church)

HUNTINGTON
Eagle Hill School - Coindre Hall
(westside of Browns Rd.)

HUNTINGTON
Coindre Hall Boat House

Continue on Browns Road to its end at Southdown Road. You can elect to go back to your car by following Southdown Road to Wall Street and south on Wall to Main Street. Left on Main for one block will take you to New York Avenue and a right on New York Avenue will take you to Route 110 to your parked car. A more scenic route that I often take is to go only a short block left on Southdown from Browns Road to John Street, right on John to West Neck Road--left on West Neck Road to Main Street. Left on Main to New York Avenue. Right turn on New York to High Street and right on High Street to Oakwood Road and left on Oakwood, crossing Jericho Turnpike to West Hills Road by way of Jones Road to your car across Route 110 behind the Walt Whitman homestead.

We have had a beautiful bike ride on roadways used by our colonial ancestores. We have enjoyed the scenery and sea breezes of Huntington, one of the loveliest areas of Long Island. We have seen homes made of hand-hewn timbers; we have seen handmade furniture and homespun cloth, and we have paid tribute to our young revolutionary hero, Nathan Hale as well as to our greatest native poet, Walt Whitman.

56

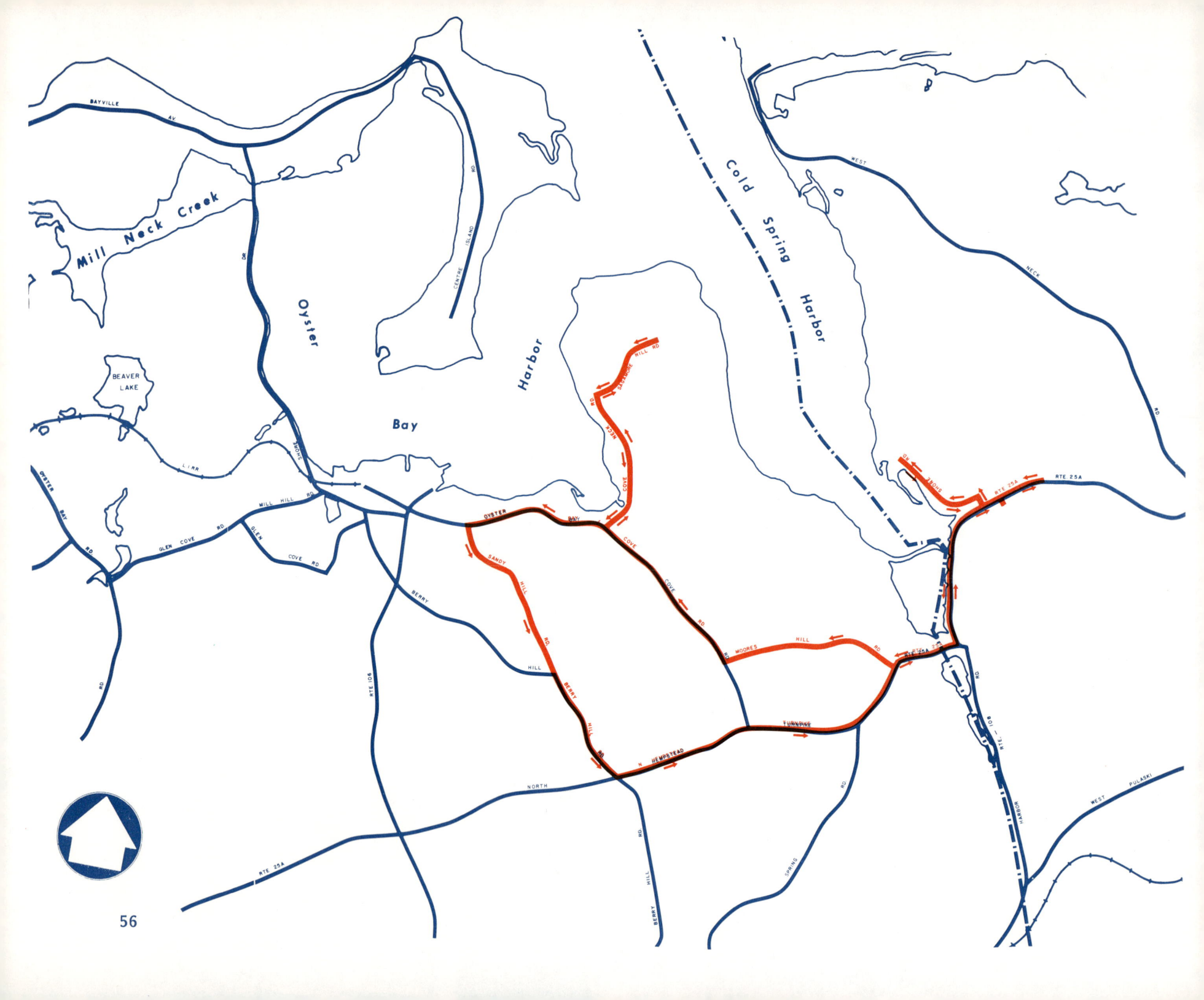

COLD SPRING HARBOR -

SAGAMORE HILL TO OYSTER BAY

Directions

Northern State Parkway to Woodbury Road (Exit 38A). North on Woodbury Road across Jericho Turnpike (N.Y. Rte. 25) to Harbor Road - North on Harbor Road to Cold Spring Harbor.

Distance

Entire bike trip and return 15 miles.
Cold Spring Harbor section only - 5 miles.

Park your car at the public parking lot on Main Street if you plan to limit this excursion to Cold Spring Harbor. If you are considering doing the entire trip to Teddy Roosevelt's house and back, you had better find a no-time-limit parking spot on a side street for this is an all day "tired when I got home" venture.

After you park your car you can proceed west on Route 25A to the firehouse garage (southside of Route 25A); turn right on Shore Road. There is no sign post at this street. Make your right turn at the firehouse garage and have a pleasant ride along the shore of Cold Spring Harbor. This road dead-ends. Return to Route 25A and go west to the Fish Hatchery and see the State of New York trout farm in action. From there bike to the Cold Spring Harbor Laboratory on the northside of Route 25A, slightly west of the Fish Hatchery.

COLD SPRING HARBOR
*Cold Spring Harbor Village
(Main St. looking east)*

COLD SPRING HARBOR
Cold Spring Harbor Library
(Main St.)

The Laboratory, under Dr. James D. Watson, the Nobel Laureate, is a research facility that is also deeply involved in teaching and publishing both its own research results and comprehensive analyses of the areas being investigated. The fields of tumor viruses, genetics, neuro-biology, human cancer, marine sciences and molecular biology are the chief fields of investigation.

Dr. Watson received the Nobel prize in 1962 for medicine and physiology. He, along with Francis H.C. Crick and Maurice H.F. Wilkins who shared in the prize determined the structure of the DNA Molecule and found it to be the double Helix. Theirs was the greatest discovery in the field of heredity since Mendel a hundred years before.

Dr. Watson, in his Director's Report (1977) gives the historical background for the Cold Spring Harbor Laboratory. He says that Science first came to Cold Spring Harbor under the patronage of John D. Jones - of the Jones family, after whom Jones Beach is named. Mr. Jones came out for the rights of slaves and had his house burned for it. He rebuilt on the same site and that grand Victorian house is now the Carnegie Dorm.

Dr. Watson tells of the Fish Hatchery started by Mr. Jones and his friend Eugene Blackford in the early 1880's. Several years later they gave funds and the land adjacent to the Hatchery for the Laboratory. It was completed in 1892 and is now called Jones Lab. Mr. Jones set up the Wawepex Society for its support; this Society has been the Lab's steadiest benefactor for the last 80 years.

Dr. Watson tells of the achievements of the Lab over the last 70 years in the booklet of the Long Island Biological Association (LIBA). It has been in the forefront in the study of hered-

COLD SPRING HARBOR
Cold Spring Harbor Fish Hatchery

58

ity and it was here that the first hybrid corn was grown in 1906. From 1920 - 1930 the inbred strains of mice that are important in cancer research were developed. Later, work was done on bacteria and their viruses, the phages, to learn about the chemical basis for heredity. This led to one of the key experiments by Alfred Hershey in 1952. which identified DNA as the genetic molecule.

The key objectives now, says Dr. Watson, are to understand how cancer cells arise and to learn the molecular features that allow them to grow uncontrolled. He says that the Lab is also interested in the functioning of nerve cells and how they form the basis for perception, memory and learning.

I quote Dr. Watson:

"Toward these aims we always strive to have in residence a powerful collection of scientists. Usually just fresh from their formal training, and often from far away parts of the world, they usually stay here for the two-to-five year periods that are generally necessary for major scientific advances. Complementing their presence are large numbers of visitors who come here to learn from one of our advanced summer courses or to take part in a meeting on a topic directly related to our own research interests. Over the past year, some two thousand different scientists were with us, and so Cold Spring Harbor remains what it has long been, one of the major centers in the world for the development of modern biology."

COLD SPRING HARBOR
Cold Spring Harbor Lab
(northside North Hempstead Turnpike)

If you decide to limit your cycling to the Fish Hatchery and the research laboratory, you could at this time return to Cold Spring Harbor for lunch. Slightly east of the Lab on Route 25A, on the southside of the road, you will find John & Ida's Whaler's Inn, which has good solid American food, well prepared and nicely served. Prices are moderate.

Just before the Town Parking Lot on the northside of Main Street is a truly gourmet restaurant, "The Country Kitchen". Here you will find specialties such as Stuffed Cabbage, Hungarian Goulash and other unusual dishes worth trying. Prices are moderate.

After lunch, go east a short distance to the Whaling Museum, open from 11:00 A.M. to 5:00 P.M. every day. (From June to September it is closed on Saturday and Sunday).

If you decide to go on to Sagamore Hill, you can proceed west along North Hempstead Turnpike (west of the Fish Hatchery) to Moores Hill Road. Take the right fork - and continue to Cove Road. (You will find this rather off the main road, traveling delightful. Be prepared for hilly, but not excessively tiring, biking). Turn right on Cove Road. Continue and you will come upon Teddy Roosevelt's Bird Sanctuary 'and Fountain. It is a good spot for a slow walk through the sanctuary and a brief rest in preparation for the ride up Sagamore Hill.

You will enjoy visiting Theodore Roosevelt's 22-room Victorian Mansion set high on the hill. It is open all year daily from 9:00 A.M. - 5:00 P.M. There is a $.50 charge for adults. It was built for him in 1884-85 and served as a summer White House from 1901 - 1909 during his presidency. The original furnishings are still there.

In addition to the house there are on the grounds a gift shop and Old Orchard Museum with audio-visual presentations of the life of Theodore Roosevelt.

He died here in 1919.

Return by way of Cove Neck Road which becomes East Main Street, Oyster Bay. Turn left at Sandy Hill Road which, in its continuation, becomes Berry Hill Road and go to North Hempstead Turnpike (Route 25A). Turn left on Route 25A to Cold Spring Harbor. A tour of Main Street with its shops of all kinds will make a restful end to a long pleasant day.

COLD SPRING HARBOR
Whaling Museum
(northside of Main St.)

OYSTER BAY
Teddy Roosevelt's Bird Sanctuary
(westside of Oyster Bay Cove Rd.)

OYSTER BAY
Sagamore Hill National Historic Site
(east end Sagamore Hill Rd.)

Roosevelt's 22 Room Victorian Mansion

OYSTER BAY
Old Orchard Museum (Sagamore Hill)

62

OYSTER BAY - OAK NECK, BAYVILLE, MILL NECK, LATTINGTOWN

Directions

Take L.I. Expressway, Exit 41 or Northern Parkway, Exit 35. Follow N.Y. Route 106 North to South Street.

Oyster Bay will, for most Americans, evoke thoughts of Theodore Roosevelt and his home. This area has been discussed in the chapter entitled "Cold Spring Harbor and Sagamore Hill". Today's journey will start at the hamlet of Oyster Bay at a pre-revolutionary house, Raynham Hall, the home of Robert Townsend. He has been identified as the mysterious Culper Jr. (his code name) of the American Secret Service, or spy corps, that General Washington established to keep informed of British troop movements when Long Island and Manhattan were occupied by British soldiers during the Revolutionary War. He and his aides uncovered Benedict Arnold's plot to turn West Point over to the British, help them gain control of the Hudson River and effect the isolation of the New England colonies.

To get to Raynham Hall, continue on South Street and turn left at the second light. It is on the right. You can park your car there and proceed with the bike tour by returning to South Street. Turn left onto West Main and then turn right on Spring Street. This will take you to Roosevelt Park. You can tour the beach and enjoy the view of Oyster Bay Harbor. Turn right in the park to a large marina. Boats, sail and power, of all sizes shapes and colors are tied up to the docks or are moored in this very secure haven. To the right is Cove Neck, the site of Sagamore Hill. Directly ahead is Center Island, a quiet residential community contiguous to and perpendicular to Bayville. To the left is Mill Neck. You will travel on the beautiful Shore Road which runs along the eastern edge of Mill Neck and crosses over Mill Neck Bay into Oak Neck. You will see areas of marsh grass, mud flats and beaches. There will be marinas and boat yards and a very active waterway.

From the park turn left on Maxwell Avenue and right on West Main Street - it becomes West Shore Road. You will have two miles of very pleasant biking, all at sea level with the waters

OYSTER BAY

Raynham Hall
(northside West Main St.)

Chain Links - Raynham Hall
(northside West Main St.)

OYSTER BAY

Teddy Roosevelt Park
(west end of Harbor Pl.)

of Oyster Bay in almost constant view. After you cross the bridge into Oak Neck, turn right on West Harbor Road. You will bike by several very busy beaches all with fine sand on the Sound and on the Bay, with Bayview Avenue separating the two bodies of water. Oysters and clams can be dug but a permit must be obtained at Town Hall if you plan to dig more than a dozen.

You can bike through Centre Island, although police at a booth guard the entrance. I biked through but saw cars stopped and the drivers questioned. The Island is moderately hilly and the homes are widely spaced and attractive. It

side trip to Mill Neck Bay. You can do this by turning left on Mountain Road which runs along the Bay. You can return to Bayville Avenue by going North on Perry Avenue. For a short distance it will again become a coast road. The first restaurant seen after the road emerges from the interior is Steve's Pier 1. It is big, well-appointed, and the motif of the sea is ever present. The front doors are flanked by a pair of magnificent 4-bladed propellers about 7 feet in diameter, painted shiny black. They are chewed out at the tips as though the channel had eluded the helmsman. Inside, the same sea decor is carried out - divers' helmets and body suits are placed at the sides of the bridge over an odd shaped indoor fish pond.

OYSTER BAY
    Centre Island
       (looking across from Roosevelt Park)

OYSTER BAY
    Mill Neck
       (looking west from Roosevelt Park)

will be necessary to retrace your path since Centre Island Road is the only road and dead ends at the southern tip. As you continue on Bayville Avenue you will arrive at an area of good restaurants and watering (or beer) stops. I like Wally's Wharf. It is directly on the Sound, has picture windows behind the bar and a pleasant, ever-changing seascape always in view. You can get cold beer bottled or drawn from the keg. I have eaten at this restaurant. The fish is fresh, tastefully broiled, and served with a loaf of hot bread. All the tables are in front of large windows. On clear days, Stamford, Connecticut can easily be seen across the Sound.

    Bayville Avenue will take you through the Village of Bayville. I would suggest taking a

OYSTER BAY

Oak Neck Bridge

Mill Neck Bay
(looking south from Shore Rd.)

OYSTER BAY

Ransom Beach
(north side Bayville Ave.)

Striped bass swim and lobsters crawl lazily on the bottom, completely unaware that they will in due course become the main course. The tables have red and white cloths, and the napkins are startling red. Everything is neat and well managed--and the view is superb. The entire north wall is on the water's edge. Shiny glass picture windows, one next to the other, extend the entire length of the large dining room. Dinners range from $12 - $14 including soup, desert and coffee. There is a complete menu of fish, fowl, and various meats; in addition, wild pheasant, bear steaks, roast wild duck or wild boar chops are served in season.

There are other restaurants nearby. Across the street the "Epicure" and the "Pig and Whistle" seem neat and well-appointed and there is a snack bar where I got three scoops of ice cream with sauce for fifty-four cents. The beach adjacent to Pier 1 extends for hundreds of feet; is very clean, has fine sand and an adequate number of life guards.

Continue riding west on Bayville Avenue. It makes a sharp left turn at a motel. There is an asphalt bike path shaded by maple, oak and locust trees. You will find Factory Pond Road about 3/4 mile south on the left. Turn down that street and have a very easy ride. There is very little traffic. Beautiful homes and estates line both sides of the road. You are now travelling in Lattington and will continue in that town until the road dead ends at Cleft Road. Turn left there and cross the Robert De Graff Causeway. A fresh water beaver dam is on the right. I am told that large mouth bass weighing over 5 pounds have been caught. On the left side of the Causeway is an arm of Mill Neck Bay. The entire area is a wildlife refuge. This road takes you through an area of landscaped gardens and manicured lawns, as well as through areas of wild woodland, ponds and grassy glens. Cleft Road dead ends at Shore Road. Turn right and you will be at your car in Oyster Bay within 10 minutes.

OYSTER BAY
Underhill Burying Grounds
(southwest side of Factory Pond Rd.)

OYSTER BAY
Beaver Lake
(looking south from Cleft Rd.)

68

BETHPAGE STATE PARK TO

JONES BEACH STATE PARK

Directions

Long Island Expressway to Exit N.Y. 36A (Seaford-Oyster Bay Expressway) Route 135, go South to Powell Avenue and follow signs to Bethpage State Park. Leave your car at the picnic grounds parking lot. You will pass the State Park Police Headquarters, a busy golf course (in season), and you will find a very large parking lot adjacent to the picnic grounds without difficulty. Be sure to return before dark since the park closes at sunset.

If time or young children make the ride to Jones Beach from Bethpage Park impractical, the round trip of about twenty-five miles can be cut in half or converted to two outings by making the Bethpage Cedar Creek Park one day, to be followed by the just as pleasant Cedar Creek Park to Jones Beach ride another day. To drive to Cedar Creek Park, use the Oyster Bay Expressway and exit at Merrick Road. Park your car under the shade of a tree on a quiet side street and be sure to write a note to yourself, tucked away in a pocket or purse, describing exactly where you parked your car. It is a little disconcerting to have to search for a car that was parked many hours before on a street whose name just slipped out of the mind. (You remember distinctly that the car was parked next to a house with purple blinds showing behind green shutters but you had forgotten to jot down the names of intersecting streets.) You can bike to Cedar Creek Park, a very short ride, by going west on Merrick Road for about one-half mile. The entrance, clearly marked, is on the south side of the road. If you arrive at the intersection of the Wantagh Parkway and Merrick Road you have gone too far and must return east about four blocks. The bike path starts at the northwestern edge of Cedar Creek Park and follows the Wantagh Parkway to Jones Beach on a delightfully curved and scenic bike path. We will pick up this ride on the way south from Bethpage Park.

Robert Moses created Bethpage State Park by getting an option to purchase about 1,300 acres of land having one golf course and a partially completed second one for $1,100,000. He got the local counties and towns which would most benefit by the development of the tract of land to contribute $30,000 to secure an option to hold the property for park purposes for one year. This option was renewed and in 1933 the "Bethpage Park Authority" was created with the members of the Long Island Park Commission in control. In

BETHPAGE
Entrance to State Park

Bethpage State Park Club House

BETHPAGE
Entrance to Old Bethpage Village Restoration

August of 1933 the owners of the land accepted $100,000 in cash and $900,000 in authority bonds (less than the option price) for the land and improvements. The $100,000 in cash was raised by the purchase of bonds by the State Controller. Title was taken in March of 1934. A new clubhouse, three additional golf courses, a polo field and other improvements were made in 1934 and 1935 as a work relief project. This resulted in the reduction of the relief rolls by 1,800 men, who were given employment there at its peak building time.

Proceed south on the Bethpage Bikeway. It is beautifully clean and smooth and free of broken glass. It meanders gently alongside a slowly flowing stream for part of its distance with tailored backyards of homes bordering it, going through East Meadow, North Merrick and Merrick.

From time to time the stream widens into a pond and boys of all ages can be seen fishing from the not too steep bank. When the bikeway crosses the Southern State Parkway be sure to stay on the bike path--it is wide and curves to the left; a narrow hard-surfaced path runs alongside a wire fence which leads off the bikeway to North Broadway, Massapequa--but continue on the bikeway; it will lead you through Roosevelt Park past a reservoir and lakes to Massapequa Railroad Station. Make a right turn here and go through the station parking lot to Broadway. Turn left (south) onto Broadway for three blocks to its end at Hicksville Road. Continue south on Hicksville Road to its end at Merrick Road. A right turn here for one and one-half miles on Merrick Road (west) will get you to Cedar Creek Park. You will see the clearly marked entrance to the park on the left side of the street. Enter the park and find the bike path to Jones Beach about 1,000 feet south on the right hand border of the park.

Jones Beach was a barren, deserted, windswept sandspit when Robert Moses first happened upon it in 1921 while exploring the Great South Bay alone in a small motor boat. He lived in Babylon at that time and the barren island-studded areas intrigued him. He transformed this almost uninhabited wasteland of sand, salt and marsh grass into one of the world's greatest oceanfront parks. It is named for Major Thomas Jones who came to Long Island in 1692 after stormy years spent supporting the deposed King James II of England.

While in France, the deposed King, with the help of French, Scotch and Irish supporters, mounted a military and naval assault in an attempt to regain his throne through an invasion of England by way of Ireland. In the resulting battle of the Boyne River, July 1, 1690, the Jacobite (James II) forces were defeated and the King and his forces returned to France.

MASSAPEQUA
Bike Path Massapequa Park

Major Jones went back to France with his defeated King and was given command of a ship outfitted for him by the French to prey on British shipping as a privateer; he was soon bottled up in the West Indies where he abandoned his ship. He proceeded to Long Island, arriving in 1692. Soon afterwards he married Freelove Townsend and settled down with his wife on vast acreage around Massapequa, given to them as a wedding gift by her father. It included all the land comprising Jones Beach, a narrow coastal barrier of sand and marsh inaccessible and rarely visited.

In 1925 Commissioner Moses, as President of the Long Island Park Commission, asked the Town of Hempstead for its interest in the outer beach and for a right of way across the great South Bay for State Park and parkway construction. In December of 1926 the first stake was driven at the site of the water tower for engineering purposes and this magnificent park was started. Building took three years and was dedicated by Major Thomas Jones on August 4, 1929.

During the war years bicycles were permitted on the causeways but as auto traffic increased it proved too hazardous and had to be stopped. The bike path from Cedar Creek State Park to Jones Beach borders the Wantagh Parkway from Merrick Road to a Jones Beach parking field. Enjoy the view from the bridges and the causeways connecting the islands where the bike path is protected by concrete barriers. You will bike from Cedar Creek Park across Great Island and then cross Green Island to the park. You will see fishing boats and clam diggers active on the water. In the shallows, thatch can be seen grey-white in the winter and shining green in the summer; and everywhere the birds can be heard in the woods, the meadows, and in the cover of thatch along the shore.

Bicycle stands to secure your bike are plentifully available at the end of the bikeway where it enters the parking field. Bikes are permitted on the boardwalk from October 1 to March 31 only. The walk from the bicycle parking area to the beach area is minimal. The Boardwalk restaurant serves lunches and dinners and I have found it most satisfactory and moderately priced.

MASSAPEQUA
Bike Path   Massapequa Park

SEAFORD
*Entrance to Cedar Creek Park
(southside of Merrick Rd.)*

I prefer to wait a bit longer and get a window table for the beach and ocean view while dining. If you parked your car at Bethpage State Park, remember to leave Jones Beach in time to get back before dark.

SEAFORD
Bike Path to Jones Beach

JONES BEACH
Jones Beach Water Tower

JONES BEACH
Map of Long Island at Jones Beach

Boardwalk Area

JONES BEACH
Flag Pole and Green

74

BROOKLYN BRIDGE AREA AND MANHATTAN FINANCIAL DISTRICT

Directions

See following paragraphs

My first long bike ride, one that I have repeated many times, to the financial district of the City of New York, is as exciting today as it was the first time that I did it. Since my trips originate at the North Shore of Long Island, I always include a ride through the Brooklyn Bridge waterfront area and a thrilling ride over the bridge itself on the way there. In addition to its being a beautiful journey, it is also the shortest route there from my home.

Those who wish to forego the Brooklyn part of the trip may drive directly to the financial district of Manhattan by proceeding south on Broadway to its end, curve left on State Street and left again onto South Street. You can park your car under the FDR Drive near the Southport Museum, where parking rates are moderate, and start your bicycle trip from there.

Those who choose to include the Brooklyn Bridge segment can, if they come from Long Island, use the Brooklyn Queens Expressway and exit at Cadman Plaza West, (exit number 28) curve under the Expressway staying on Cadman Plaza West to Henry Street, turn right onto Henry Street and continue to Clark Street - make another right turn onto Clark Street and proceed to Columbia Heights. Parking space is usually available on Columbia Heights or a nearby street.

If you decide to include this part of Brooklyn, walk the bike down to the promenade and enjoy the view of the East River, Manhattan and points North, West and South. After a tour of the Promenade, on foot, since bicycle riding is not permitted, go back to Columbia Heights, mount your bike and turn left to the waterfront.

Visit the Fulton Ferry Museum (hours - Noon to 6:00 P.M. daily). Spend some minutes at the Barge Music Promenade (Chamber music on Sunday afternoon), lean on the balustrade and enjoy the view. From here you can watch the loading and unloading of freighters at the Port Authority docks.

BROOKLYN
Barge Music Cafe

BROOKLYN
Fulton Ferry Museum

MANHATTAN
Lower Manhattan Skyline

Adjacent to Barge Music is the delightful River Cafe, a Breath of the Left Bank of Paris. The cafe is a nicely rebuilt barge set onto a landscaped dock with outdoor tables placed so that every table has a view of lower Manhattan. Here you can sit, enjoy lunch and watch the busy harbor traffic. Indoors there are large picture windows overlooking the harbor. The diners with their backs to the windows can watch the active waterfront because of skillfully placed mirrors. Service is good and decor is pleasing as is the piano music by Michael. The scenes are unending.

Return to Cadman Plaza and go to Prospect Street. Go left one block. Turn right to Cadman Plaza East. The entrance to the Brooklyn Bridge is on the right under the bridge itself. The bike must be carried up a fairly long flight of stairs and steps with ramps will be encountered at intervals. A word of caution: there have been newspaper accounts of molestation of bike riders on the bridge, but I have not experienced any trouble on any of my trips.

At the end of the bridge, at the first traffic light, cross over to City Hall Park and bear left to Pace University. Go down Spruce Street to Gold Street, then turn left to Fulton Street. Go on until you smell the fish market. Spend some time at the Southport Museum. See the old sailing ships and the Hospital ship and enjoy the view.

MANHATTAN
Rejected Skin By William Tarr

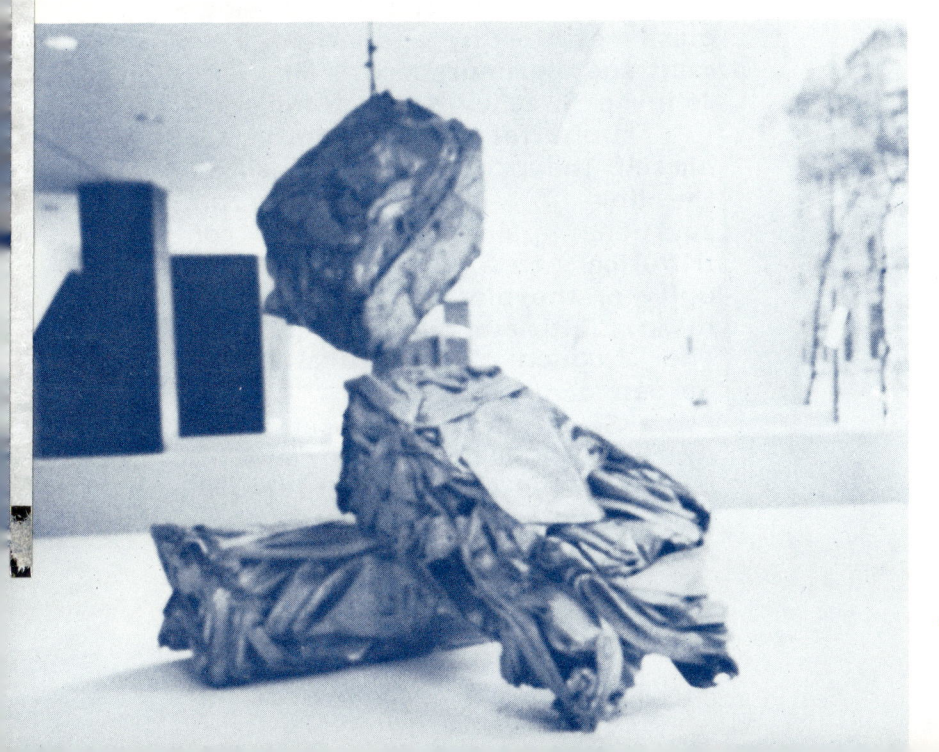

MANHATTAN
Clock on John St.

Proceed west on John Street. You will see a full wall panel divided into squares with moving lights. It is a clock. The lights define the hours, the minutes and the seconds.

Turn south (left) on Water Street and notice the promenade and plaza at 77 Water Street. Notice also the old fashioned candy store. Examine the sculptures: "Rejected Skin" by William Tarr, on the southwest corner; "City Fountains" by Victor Scallo on the northwest corner; and "Month of June" by George Adamy on the southeast corner.

From 77 Water Street, proceed south to Pine Street. There you will find Chase Manhattan Plaza, the most beautiful plaza in the financial district. It is dominated by Jean Dubuffet's sculpture, "Group of Four Trees."

City Fountains By Victor Scallo

MANHATTAN

Month of June by George Adamy

David Rockefeller said of the "Group of Four Trees" that the Chase Bank's art committee had decided that a major work of art was needed to dominate the 2 1/2 acre plaza that would surround the world's largest bank building. They had already commissioned Isamu Noguchi to design a sunken water garden on the southeast corner. They felt that the broad open areas remaining needed a vertical counterpoint. For more then ten years the problem was studied until finally in 1970 the committee selected Jean Dubuffet to do a work in his L'Hourloupe style.

"This creation was fabricated at the artist's workshop at Perigny-Sur-Yerres, near Paris. It was then disassembled, shipped to New York and reexecuted in the plaza by a team from M. Dubuffet's atalier. It is the largest sculpture in New York, rising 42 feet above the plaza. Its exterior is a fiberglass resin skin, applied to a cement and aluminum core." Mr. James Johnson Sweeney says of the work:

"Dubuffet as a sculptor, set himself the problem of intensifying the link of a building to its plaza...The painter-sculptor's contribution ties the architectural unity of the plaza and building into an...intimate relationship."
The Noguchi Sculptural Water Garden consists of:

"Seven natural basalt rocks which dominate the pool's contoured base of 27,000 gray-white granite blocks. The sculptor selected the rocks from the Uji River bed in

78

Kyoto, Japan, where they had been eroded into distinctive shapes by centuries of exposure to rushing, sandladen water. They weigh from 1 1/2 to 7 1/2 tons each and vary in height, the largest standing at about 6 feet.

After shipment from Japan, the huge rocks were positioned by metal hoists under Mr. Noguchi's supervision. A concrete supporting base was poured as each rock was placed in an abstract pattern.

Near the center of the pool is a large fountain of 45 vertical pipes set in angular concentric patterns. The fountain can produce a massive spray, a bubbling effect, or anything in between. Two of the rocks have been drilled for water pipes to produce a waterfall effect.

When the pool's water is turned on during warm weather, water lilies float on the surface as water slowly spills into an encircling trough at the edge of the pool. In the winter months, when the pool is drained, juniper shrubs are planted in the area.

From Ann Van Camp's -
ARCHIVES OF CHASE MANHATTAN BANK

MANHATTAN
Group of Four Trees by Jean Dubuffets

MANHATTAN
Legion Park on Louise Nevelson Plaza

Slightly north of the Chase Manhattan Plaza you will find Legion Park, a small, triangular park with Callery pear trees, benches, and a brick walk, all dominated by seven sculptural works by Louise Nevelson. This vest-pocket park, bounded by Maiden Lane, Liberty and Williams Streets is a gem amidst the towering structures of the financial district. The art works it contains are companions to those at the Chase Manhattan Plaza. "The steel black painted sculptures are placed on masts and appear to float like flags."

NEW YORK TIMES.

During lunch hour, this park, also called the Louise Nevelson Plaza, is a magnet drawing groups of friends and onlookers who use this space so beautifully designed for meeting, rest and companionship.

The sculptures, the gift of an anonymous donor to the City, were placed on land, owned by the City, which had been cleared several years before as part of a plan to widen Liberty Street. Construction costs, as well as maintenance and security costs, are covered by businesses in the area.

As you proceed south, notice the plaza and mall at 55 Water Street and the old fashioned diner at Pearl and Fletcher Streets.

Go south on Pearl Street through the heart of the financial quarter and return north on Broad Street until it merges with Nassau Street. See Federal Hall. The current name commemorates the building, on the same site, in which Washington took the oath of office as President in 1789. The statue of Washington stands on the approximate spot where the oath was administered. The building contains interesting exhibits. You should lock up your bike and go inside.

Notice the New York Stock Exchange. The pediment was sculptured by the John Quincy Adams Ward who also did the Washington figure in front of Federal Hall.

If you desire to go through the Stock Exchange Building, avail yourself of one of the guided tours.

Continue north on Nassau Street and circle City Hall Park, then go south on Broadway and see St. Paul's Chapel. It is the oldest church building in Manhattan (1764-66). It is also the only pre-revolutionary building in the City of New York that is basically still intact.

Continue south, and at the corner of Wall Street and Broadway see Trinity Church, built in 1864. (It is the third Trinity Church on this site. The first, raised in 1698, lasted until 1776, when it was destroyed by fire. The second, built in 1790, was demolished in 1839). Alexander Hamilton and Robert Fulton are buried in the churchyard.

As you continue south on Broadway, you will come to the Marine Midland Bank building at the corner of Liberty Street. In its plaza there is a large red cube standing on end, the work of Noguchi (who also did the Sculpture Water Garden previously mentioned at the Chase Manhattan Building). This startlingly immense cube, with a hole through its center that is lined with stainless steel strips seems to defy gravity. Most people walk around it to discover what is holding it up.

The beautiful vest-pocket parks, plazas and sculptures mentioned are not a complete list. You will find many more by browsing through the financial district. Nowhere in the City of New York will you find so much that is beautiful in so small an area.

MANHATTAN
Noguchi Red Cube on End
(Marine Midland Bank)

Three Red Wings by Calder

MANHATTAN

Old Watson House

MANHATTAN
Customs House with Sculptures

Continue along Broadway and view the U.S. Customs House. Built in 1907 it has four monumental sculptures, part of the facade, which represent America, Asia, Africa and Europe - also the work of John Quincy Adams' Ward.

Nestled into a curve facing the Battery is the beautiful old Watson House, now Our Lady of the Rosary Roman Catholic Church. It was built in 1800, when many mansions occupied the then fashionable thoroughfare. It has been declared a landmark of New York City.

Continue north along West Street to the World Trade Center.

Beautiful sculptures have done for New York City what the fountains have done for Rome - made the city memorable.

A red painted steel stabile, "Three Red Wings" by Alexander Calder stands at the West Street side of the World Trade Center and in the Plaza are three superb sculptures.

At the Church Street entrance stands Masayuke Nagare's massive black granite work executed in Japan. The pyramidal sculpture of Swedish granite is 34 feet long, 14 feet high, and 17 feet wide. The Nagare's black hue contrasts pleasantly with the white Paridiso stone imported from Italy to make up the Plaza paving.

As one approaches the center of the Plaza, the focal point within a 90-foot diameter fountain area is the Fritz Koenig bronze "free form" globe by the noted artist/sculptor from Munich, Germany. The 25-foot-high globe, which weighs 17 tons, ultimately will revolve slowly in the center of the fountain at the rate of one revolution per hour, as the water rises in graceful sprays three feet above the black granite base on which the sculpture rests.

MANHATTAN
Black Granite by Nagare

The third Plaza sculpture is the commission of James Rosati, an American artist/sculptor now residing in New York City. Known as "Ideogram," it is comprised of 1/4-inch highly polished stainless steel, some 28 feet in length, 23 feet high and 18 feet in diameter. The modern work occupies a prominent area between the two Tower Buildings, near the West Street entrance to the Plaza.

    Publicity Office
    PORT AUTHORITY OF NEW YORK AND
                 NEW JERSEY

MANHATTAN
Rosati Ideogram

Do not neglect a tour through and around Battery Park, with its unobstructed view of the Bay. You can see the Statue of Liberty, Governor's Island and Ellis Island. Watch the boats - cargo ships, tour ships, trans-atlantic liners, and the beetle-like ferries bustling on their way to Staten Island. Walk into Castle Clinton - which was first a fort, then an aquarium - and now is a national landmark restored to its original form.

North of Battery Park is the clearing and filled land for Battery Park City. This land was created by the filling-in of the Hudson River dock area from Battery Park to Chambers Street. The entire project consists of 88 acres of filled-in land plus 16 acres to be made by depressing the West Side Highway and building a platform over it.

In 1968 Governor Rockefeller and Mayor Lindsay agreed to the creation of a non-profit corporation to build a $1.1 billion residential community, which was to be the largest single urban development in U.S. history and was to include office space, housing, schools, shops, theatres, restaurants, hotels and parks. It was also to have its own internal transportation system.

During the decade from 1968-78, the Battery Park City Authority dumped the fill necessary to form the land upon which the project was to be built, creating this country's most expensive empty lot. A combination of unfortunate events led to the stasis of the Battery Park City building program. In 1968, the estimate for the project was $1.1 billion; in 1978 it was increased to $1.5 billion, an additional $400,000,000. If part of that $1.5 billion projected expenditure had been put into the renovation of the No-man's land south of Stuyvesant Town, that area between 14th and Houston Streets, could have been opened up into a livable district large enough to entice back to the City some of the middle class that left it years ago.

To get construction started at Battery Park City, Governor Carey and Mayor Koch signed a new agreement in November of 1979 and a new tax plan was written in October of 1981. In mid-1982, the steel skeletons of two buildings show promise of things to come. There is hope now that Battery Park City will roll off the drawing boards and onto the beautiful site created for it.

Turn right on Chambers Street. Notice the Woolworth Building at the corner of Barclay Street and Broadway now in the process of renovation. It is one of the most dramatic and imposing skyscrapers in New York, with its Gothic details and its sheer mass rising 800 feet from the street.

Curve around City Hall Park and return over the Brooklyn Bridge.

ROOSEVELT ISLAND TO MANHATTAN
TO WILLIAMSBURGH, BROOKLYN

Directions

From Long Island, take the Grand Central Parkway, exit after the sign indicating the toll station at the approach to the Triboro Bridge, Hoyt Avenue. Make the first possible left turn. This will be 31st Street. It has an elevated railroad and is crowded. To get away from the congestion, turn right after a few blocks and then left onto a parallel street. Continue on to 36th Avenue, then turn right. In a short time you will see the purple bridge to Roosevelt Island.

Enter a garage called "Motorgate," and park only in the visitor's section. Your bicycle ride begins here. Turn right when you leave the garage and seek out the waterfront perimeter walkways and roads. The walkways are interrupted from time to time but almost the entire island, except for a small southern section, can be travelled at or near the water's edge. You will see Long Island City and "Big Allis" a Con Ed Plant on the right. At the northern tip the small stone lighthouse, unfortunately marred by graffitti, is set into a newly built park not quite finished at this writing, but far enough along to show that it was designed and executed with competence. The walkways are of interlocking bricks, muted tan and most attractive. The trees and ornamental plantings are in place, as are the wide rounded well-positioned benches. The view from Lighthouse Point north includes the Triboro Bridge, South Bronx and Hell's Gate, the waterway connecting Long Island Sound and the Harbor.

MANHATTAN
Bridge to Roosevelt Island - 36th Ave.

MANHATTAN
Motor Gate - Roosevelt Island

The current runs fiercely in one direction or the other as the tide rises and falls. Boats are warned to wait for the slack, the period of high or low tide when, for a brief interval, the strength of the current eases. Across the River, you will see the double-tiered FDR Drive and the park above it. Apartment houses with landscaped penthouses dominate the entire area. The wide concrete break water around Lighthouse Point is ideal for sitting, watching river traffic, looking west to Manhattan, and north into the current of Hell's Gate.

As you bike south on the western edge of the Island, the unique, impressive skyline of Manhattan unfolds and on a clear day individual skyscrapers, the Chrysler Building, the United Nations, the Empire State Building, the Woolworth Building and even the Twin Towers of the World Trade Center can be seen clearly. The shore path is interrupted and you will pass two very large

Big Allis Con Ed Power Plant

MANHATTAN

Manhattan
(from west side of Roosevelt Island)

hospitals. Roosevelt Island, at one time, was called Welfare Island, because its hospitals cared for the indigent chronically ill of the City. A reminder of past days is the shell of a hospital for the treatment of small pox, at the southern tip. More vestiges of the past are a beautiful Gothic church and other buildings now unused and disintegrating - the route has taken you into the interior - you can travel back to the western edge after you pass a fenced-in construction area. The new part of Roosevelt Island begins here; it was taken over in 1970 by the Urban Development Corporation whose plan was to create a new city with no automobile traffic. They succeeded admirably.

Notice the Chapel of the Good Shepherd between the apartment buildings. It originally was an Episcopal Church, built in 1889, and donated in 1969 to the Urban Development Corporation for use as an Ecumenical House of Worship and is a registered landmark. Take the time necessary to bike around the apartment complex, see the schools, the recreational facilities that include a gymnasium and a large indoor pool, and the park lands with well kept lawns and benches. The last time I was there the weather was hot and the lawns were decorated by many sun bathers.

Before the City of New York took over the Island for welfare purposes, it was farmed by the Blackwell family and was called Blackwell's Island. You can see the farm house, built in 1804, in "Blackwell Park" on the east side of Main Street, south of the Eastwood Apartment complex. There are stores, restaurants, and a "Grog" Shop of no mean proportion. The entire area is well kept and attractive.

Further south and nearby is the tramway to 60th Street. Bikes are permitted and there is an elevator for the aged, the infirm and bicycles. Ask the attendant to direct you, or you will have difficulty finding it. The cable car ride is short, lovely and soaring and the Manhattan skyline zooms in quickly. At the near right, Pan-Am maintains a very active heliport. Copters are in flight or landing constantly. Next you will see a beautiful house on 61st Street. Its symmetrical stone wings are connected by a white covered porch above the entrance way. Its landscaped gardens and lawns leap into view. It is the Abigail Adams Smith House, built in 1799 as the coach house and stable of an estate. It was planned by Colonel William S. Smith and was to be ready in time for his projected marriage to Abigail Adams, daughter of John Adams. Because of financial reverses only this building was completed and the grand estate was cancelled. It is now the headquarters of the Colonial Dames of America and is open to the public.

The world of the City is now wide open. It would take many volumes to outline all the bike rides that could be taken using 59th Street as

MANHATTAN
Chapel of the Good Shepherd

MANHATTAN
Blockwells Forum House

the starting point. I have used this route on many occasions and have enjoyed all the trips, which have ranged from short rides down one avenue across town and up another avenue, to rides that encompassed Midtown Manhattan, the Village, Staten Island and Brooklyn. The ride that I am outlining here is an enjoyable one, but it can be abbreviated or changed if you wish.

From here bike west to 5th Avenue. Be sure to go with, rather than against, traffic and keep to the left (on the driver's side). At 5th Avenue and Central Park south, ride through the Plaza Hotel square and take an extra turn around the Pulitzer fountain facing it. Continue down 5th Avenue - stop and look at some of the displays in store windows: Steuben Glass at 56th Street, Saks at 50th, Lord & Taylor at 39th, Altman's at 34th, to name a few. The bike ride south on 5th Avenue is great - traffic is all jammed up and you just amble on through. When you get to 23rd Street, bear to the right so that you avoid getting side tracked onto Broadway. Just before 5th Avenue ends at the Washington Square Arch, you will see Washington Mews, small houses or studios that were the stables for the large houses facing Washington Square Park. These were built in 1832.

You have now entered Greenwich Village. This is a geographic area with somewhat flexible boundaries. Fifth Avenue is on one side and Greenwich Street on the opposite. Fourth Street, with a curve down to Morton Street, is another boundary, and Thirteenth Street roughly squares it off. But it is more than a geographic area. The Village is a state of mind, a way of life - it has a tempo of its own. It is a magnet that attracts poets, painters, musicians, students and all those free spirits who find this city within the city much to their liking. Washington Square is the excentric hub.

MANHATTAN
Abigail Adams Smith House